Python Programming for Absolute Beginners

Learn Python Fast with Real-World Examples and Practical Exercises - Your Essential Guide to Confident Coding and Kickstarting Your Tech Career!

William Stenberg

Book and Cover Design: Raphael A.

Printed in the United States of America

ISBN-13 : 9798343442274

First Edition: September 2024

ACKNOWLEDGMENT

To my dear son and student, Jacob.

Every time I see your smile, I am reminded of the joy and inspiration you bring into my life, both as a father and now as your teacher. Your enthusiasm and curiosity make every day brighter and every lesson a journey of discovery.

PREFACE TO THE FIRST EDITION

Hello and welcome to the first edition of this book! I am truly grateful for the opportunity to share my knowledge and passion for Python programming with you. As my first publication, the journey to bring this book to life has been both exhilarating and challenging.

The decision to write this book came from a desire to make Python accessible to those completely new to programming. Throughout my teaching and coding experience, I've seen the need for a straightforward guide that simplifies the complexities of coding for beginners. This book aims to meet that need by providing clear, concise, and beginner-friendly explanations of fundamental Python concepts.

Since the world of Python is constantly evolving, this edition covers the latest stable version of Python, ensuring that you are learning the most up-to-date practices and features. Though this is an introductory guide, I've made sure to include a variety of examples and exercises to not only teach the basics but also to spark your curiosity about advanced topics you might explore in the future.

I recommend using the standard Python IDE as your integrated development environment to get started. It's well-suited for beginners and fully capable of handling all the exercises included in this book.

Each chapter has been carefully crafted to ensure clarity and ease of understanding, with added features like syntax highlighting to improve readability—especially for those who are new to programming. This book will provide you with a solid foundation, preparing you to dive into more specialized areas like web development, data analysis, or even AI.

A heartfelt thank you goes to my family for their endless support, my friends for their constructive feedback, and my students, whose enthusiasm and eagerness to learn continually inspire me. Your collective support has been invaluable in making this book a reality.

Best regards,
William Stenberg

CONTENTS

INTRODUCTION

Welcome to the beginning of your Python journey! If you've ever been curious about how your favorite apps, websites, or even games come to life, you're about to unlock the secrets behind them. Python is more than just a programming language; it's your key to creating, building, and exploring the digital world.

This book is designed for anyone who's eager to learn, whether you're completely new to programming or have dabbled in code before. We'll start with the very basics—no prior experience is required. By the time you reach the final chapter, you'll be well-equipped to tackle real-world programming challenges with confidence.

Why Python? Because it's simple, powerful, and incredibly versatile. It's like the Swiss Army knife of programming languages—whether you want to automate everyday tasks, dive into data analysis, or develop your own apps, Python makes it all possible. Plus, it's used by some of the biggest tech companies in the world, so you'll be in great company.

Throughout this book, I'll guide you step-by-step, making sure each concept is clear and understandable. We'll start by setting up Python on your device and writing your first lines of code. From there, we'll explore the building blocks of Python, from variables and data types to loops and functions. I'll also throw in some hands-on exercises to help you practice and reinforce what you've learned.

But this isn't just about learning to code—it's about learning to think like a programmer. You'll start seeing problems differently, breaking them down into manageable pieces, and finding creative solutions. And trust me, there's nothing quite like the feeling of watching your code come to life.

So, let's get started. Grab your device, get comfortable, and let's dive into the exciting world of Python. By the end of this journey, I promise you'll be amazed at what you can do. Welcome to the world of programming—let's make something incredible together!

1

FIRST STEP IN PROGRAMMING

A computer program is like a recipe. It is a list of steps that tells the computer how to perform a specific task or solve a problem. Following each instruction one by one on the computer, like you would follow a recipe for baking cake.

For example, let us consider your daily routine: you wake up, brush your teeth first, eat breakfast, go to school and finally come back home. How you spend your day has some kind of similarity in it. Consequently, the program itself has its own sequence of operations. It might be followed by opening file, making some changes to it and then saving it again. The same way that every day ends with sleep for you is how the program concludes its activities.

What is Programming?

Think of a computer as a really helpful friend who's not very smart. This friend wants to help you, but you need to tell them exactly what to do. This is where programming comes in. Programming is like giving your computer friend a list of instructions. Every time you click something or type a command, you're telling your computer friend what to do next.

But your computer friend takes everything literally and doesn't understand anything unless you explain it in a language they know. That's what programming languages are for. They help you talk to your computer so you can make it do all sorts of things, like play a game or show a website. We can say programming is the process of writing instructions for a computer to perform specific tasks.

What is a Programming Language?

Imagine you're trying to teach your dog to sit. You can't just say, "Hey, I'd like you to sit down now," because your dog doesn't understand English in that way. You use a specific command, like "Sit!", and maybe a hand gesture. The same goes for computers. They're really good at following instructions, but first, you need to speak their language.

A programming language is how we tell computers what we want them to do. Just like you might use English to talk to your friends and maybe another language at home, computers have their own languages like Python, Java, or C++. When you learn one of these languages, you can start telling your computer to do things. Maybe you'll tell it to create a game, help solve a math problem, or build a website. So, learning a programming language is like learning how to give commands to your computer, just like you would with a trained dog.

Benefits of Learning Programming

Learning programming is a lot like setting out on an exciting adventure where you get to be the creator. I know reading might not be your favorite thing, but imagine this: instead of just playing computer games, you can create your own! Imagine building something that moves or lights up, not just with batteries and motors, but with your ideas and code.

By learning how to program, you're not just learning to make software or games. It's about firing up your creativity and sharpening your critical thinking. When you program, you're constantly solving puzzles and figuring out new ways to do things. This kind of thinking doesn't just help in programming; it helps in real life too. You learn to look at problems differently and find smart solutions.

So, think of programming as a tool, not just for building games or apps, but for building your ability to think creatively and make smart decisions. It's about learning a skill that's fun, challenging, and really useful at the same time.

Why Python?

Among all the languages you could choose, why would you pick Python? It's simple!

- Elegance: Python's syntax is clean, clear, and readable. It's almost like reading English!

- Versatility: From web development to AI, Python can do it all.

- Community: Python boasts one of the largest and most supportive communities. You're never alone on your Python journey!

- Beginner-Friendly: Its simplicity and readability make it a great starting point for budding programmers.

Why choose Python? Python is user-friendly and versatile, making it a suitable choice for beginners and experts in programming.

Stay tuned for the next chapter where we will begin with basic Python programming exercises.

2

INSTALLING PYTHON

W e're going to get a Python for our house. We'll play with it and have lots of fun. But don't worry; this Python isn't a snake. It's something special for our computer. It's a way for the computer to learn a new language, just like we learn to read and write. When we put Python on our computer, it can understand and do new, exciting things!

Installing Python on Computer Devices

This guide aims to provide a systematic approach to installing Python, a powerful programming language, on your computer. Please follow the steps below carefully to ensure a successful installation.

Step 1: Navigate to Python's Official Website

Open your web browser and go to the official Python website at python.org.

Step 2: Access the Downloads Section

Once you're on Python's homepage, navigate to the "Downloads" section. Select the version of Python that is compatible with your operating system—Windows, macOS, or Linux.

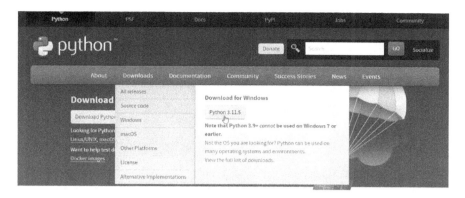

Step 3: Download and Run the Installer

After selecting the appropriate version, click to download the installer. Once the download is complete, locate the installer file and run it to initiate the installation process.

Step 4: Add Python to PATH

During the installation, you'll see an option that says "Add Python to PATH." Make sure to check this box. This is crucial as it allows you to run Python from the Command Prompt or Terminal.

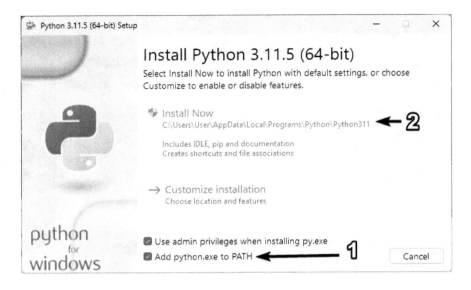

Step 5: Complete the Installation

After ensuring that the "Add Python to PATH" option is checked, proceed to complete the installation. Once the installation is successful, you should see a screen confirming the installation.

Steps to Check if Python is Installed

Step 1: Open Command Prompt

Press Windows Key + R to open the 'Run' dialog box.

Type cmd and press Enter.

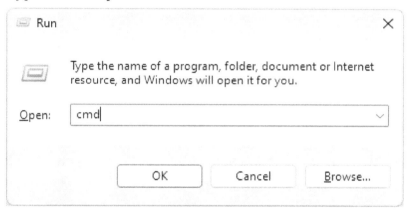

Step 2: Check Python Version:

In the Command Prompt window, type the following command python --version and press Enter.

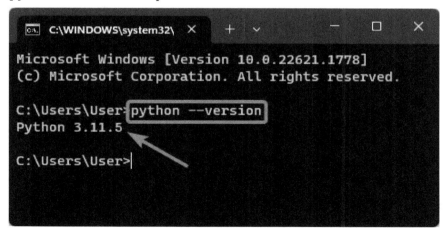

Step 3: Read the Output:

If Python is installed, this command should return the version of Python currently on your system. It will look something like this: Python 3.11.5

If you see this output, it means Python is installed correctly.

Following these steps should successfully install Python on your computer, allowing you to begin your journey into programming.

Installing Python on Your Mobile Device

This guide aims to assist you in installing Python on your mobile phone. Depending on your operating system—Android or iOS—there are different apps available to run Python code. Please follow the detailed steps below for your specific mobile platform.

For Android Users

Step 1: Open the Google Play Store

Step 2: Search for 'Pydroid 3'

In the Google Play Store search bar, enter 'Pydroid 3' and hit 'Search'.

Step 3: Install 'Pydroid 3'

Select 'Pydroid 3' from the list and tap on 'Install' to download and install the app on your device.

For iOS Users

Step 1: Open the App Store

On your iOS device, open the App Store app.

Step 2: Search for 'Pythonista'

Instructions: In the App Store search bar, type 'Pythonista' and hit 'Search'.

Description: A screenshot displaying the search results for 'Pythonista' in the App Store.

Step 3: Install 'Pythonista'

Select 'Pythonista' from the list and tap on 'Get' or 'Install' or purchase to download and install the app on your device.

Following these steps should enable you to successfully install Python on your mobile device, allowing you to program on the go.

Using Online Python Environments: No Installation Required

For those who prefer not to install any software on their computers, there are several online platforms available that allow you to write, execute, and share Python code. This guide will introduce you to two such platforms: Replit and Google Colab.

Using Replit

Step 1: Navigate to Replit Website

Open your web browser and navigate to https://replit.com/ and sign up using your email.

Step 2: Create a New Python Repl

On the replit homepage, look for an option to create a new "Repl" and select Python as the language.

Using Google Colab

Step 1: Navigate to Google Colab Website

Open your web browser and navigate to https://colab.google/

Step 2: Create a New Python Notebook

On the Google Colab homepage, look for an option to create a new "Notebook" and ensure that it is set to use Python.

Both Replit and Google Colab offer robust platforms for running Python code online without requiring any installation. These options are especially useful for those who wish to quickly try out Python code without the commitment of installing software.

The IDLE: Your Digital Python Notebook

We've already discussed IDLE, but what exactly is it? Imagine using a notepad for writing in English or a fresh white page for your math problems. Similarly, for writing Python code, there's a special "notepad" called IDLE. However, it's not something you can physically touch; it's software where you can write and run Python code. There are several environments like IDLE, including VS Code and PyCharm, which are also known as Interpreters.

Now, you might wonder, what is an interpreter? As I mentioned before, computers don't understand our language; they only understand binary, which is comprised of 0s and 1s. An interpreter converts our code into this binary format so the computer can understand it.

When it comes to saving Python code, we use the .py file extension, similar to how we use .mp3 for audio files and .mp4 for video files. This helps in easily identifying and managing Python scripts among various types of files.

Installing VS Code and Setting Up for Python

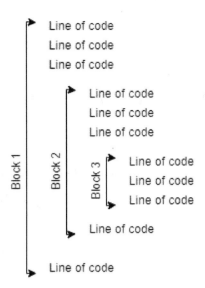

Step 1: Download and Install

Visit the Visual Studio Code website and download the installer for your operating system.

Step 2: Run the Installer

Run the installer and follow the on-screen instructions to install Visual Studio Code.

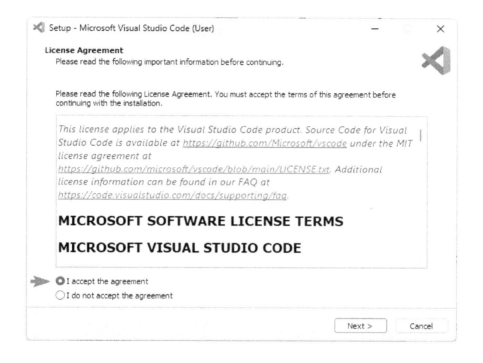

Step 3: Launch VS Code and Install Python Extension

Open VS Code, go to the Extensions Marketplace by clicking on the Extensions icon in the Activity Bar on the side of the window.

Search for "Python" and install the extension provided by Microsoft.

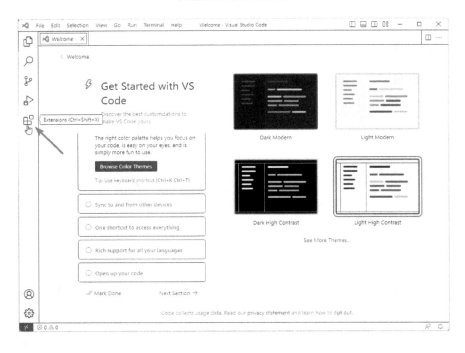

Step 4: Configure Python Interpreter

Open the Command Palette by pressing Ctrl+Shift+P or Cmd+Shift+P for macOS, and type "Python: Select Interpreter."

Choose the Python interpreter you want to use for your Python projects.

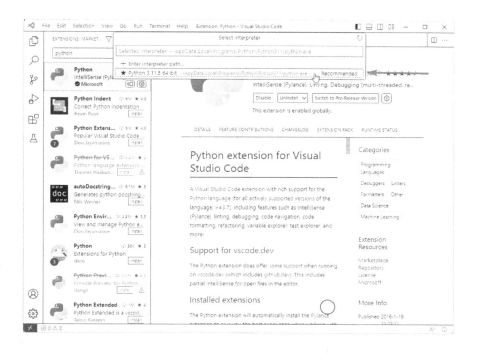

And you're set! Now, you have VS Code installed and configured for Python development. You can now create a folder and create a file with .py extension and ready to code.

3

The A B C D s of P y t h o n

W elcome back. Today, we unravel the ABCDs of Python, where A stands not for Apple, but for "Amazing" things you can do with simple commands!

Variable: Container for Storing Value

Think of a variable in Python like an empty box, ready to be filled with various items. Just like you would put toys, books, or snacks into a box, you can store data in a Python variable. In this example, the variable is the empty box, and the value is the specific item you place inside it.

```
box = "cake"
print(box)
```
Output: cake

In this example, box = "cake" is like saying you've put a cake into a box. Here, box is a variable, and "cake" is the value you're storing in it.

The print(box) part is like opening the box and showing the world what's inside. When you run this code, Python will display the words "cake" on the screen because that's the value stored in the variable box. Tomorrow, it could hold a "chocolate"!

Constants

Some things are eternal, and unchanging, like the North Star. Constants in Python are similar; once set, they remain steadfast.

```
PI = 3.1416
print(PI)
```
Output: 3.1416

Python doesn't actually have constants, or variables that you're not supposed to change. But sometimes we want to make sure a variable stays the same. So, we write the name in all capital letters. This is like a big sign saying "Don't change me!" Even though you could change it, it's a clue that you really shouldn't.

Case Sensitivity

In Python, 'Box' and 'box' are two distinct creatures. For instance, the name 'Box' with an uppercase 'B' and 'box' with a lowercase 'b' are considered two completely separate entities by Python. This characteristic of Python is known as case sensitivity.

It emphasizes the importance of consistent letter casing, as even a minor change can lead to entirely different interpretations. Always be mindful of this when naming variables or comparing strings in Python.

```
Box = "mighty beast"
box = "tiny lizard"

print(Box)
```
Output: mighty beast

```
Box = "mighty beast"
box = "tiny lizard"

print(box)
```
Output: tiny lizard

Mind your cases, or you might summon the wrong creature!

Code Block & Indentation

In Python, a colon (:) means you're starting something new, like a list of instructions. The lines that come after it need to be indented, or moved over a bit to the right. Think of it like setting up a bookshelf: the colon says, "Here's a new shelf," and the indented lines are like books you put on that shelf in a neat row.

Some programming languages use special symbols like {} to show where a new list of instructions starts and ends. But Python makes it easier. All you need to do is indent your lines so they line up nicely, just like you would line up books on a shelf.

```
# First block
if x > y:
    print("x is greater")

    # second block
    if x == 10:
        print("x is 10")

# first block
elif x == y:
    print("x and y are equal")
```

We've used two main blocks of code here. Each block starts with an **if** condition. Inside each block, the actions that should happen based on the condition need to be indented to show they're part of that block.

Failure to indent correctly will result in a syntax error in Python.

Here's an example showcasing three code blocks:

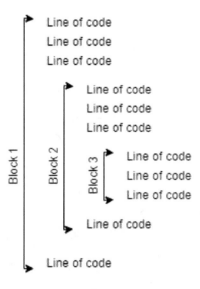

To understand conditions, loops, functions, etc., we need a clear understanding of code blocks or indentation.

Comments in Code

Comments are like little notes you leave in your code to explain what's going on. Imagine you're reading a book but forget what happened in the last chapter; comments are like bookmarks that help you remember. This is really handy when you look at your code days or weeks later and need to remember what you were thinking.

Also, if someone else needs to read your code, like a teammate or a teacher, these comments help them understand what you've done. Imagine you join a group project, and they've already started the coding. If they've used comments, it's easier for you to catch up and understand what the code is doing. The best part? These comments don't affect how your program runs at all, because Python ignores them when running your code.

```
# This is a secret note. Python will ignore this!
print("Python hears this!")
```
Output: Python hears this!

Identifiers

Identifiers are basically the names you give to things in your code, like how you name your folders on your computer so you know what's inside. You've got variables, functions, and classes, and each needs its own name so you can find it easily later. It's kind of like calling someone "Doctor" because they're in medicine, or "Teacher" because they teach.

So if you have a variable that holds someone's age, you might just name it "age" to keep things simple and clear. This way, you and anyone else who reads your code will know what that variable is for.

```
age = 20
print(age)
```
Output: 20

The Sacred Naming Conventions

In Python, there are traditional ways to name things in your code. Following these naming conventions helps make your code easier to read and understand.

snake_case: Use lowercase letters and underscores for variables and functions. For example, "speed_limit".

CamelCase: Use an uppercase letter to start each word for class names, like "TotalCount".

It's good practice to follow these conventions. Think of them as age-old traditions that keep everything in harmony!

Forbidden Words: Keywords

In Python, some words like "if," "else," and "print" are special and already have a job to do. So, you can't use them to name your own stuff like variables. Think of them as VIP words that are already booked for special tasks.

input()

Imagine your phone's password screen—you type in the password, hit enter, and then your phone unlocks. This is like giving input to your phone. In Python, we have a function called input() that does something similar.

So, when you see input() in Python, think of it as a way to ask the person using your program for some information. Just like your phone waits for you to enter the password, the input() function waits for you to type something and press enter. Whatever you type becomes the input that your program can work with. It's a way to make your program interactive!

```python
box_name = input("What should we call this secret box? ")
print(f"We'll call it: {box_name}")
```

box_name = input("What should we call this secret box? ")

Here, we're using the 'input()' function to ask the user a question: "What should we call this secret box?" The user can type an answer, and whatever they type will be stored in the 'box_name' variable. It's like having a conversation with the program!

print(f"We'll call it: {box_name}")

This line uses the 'print()' function to show a message on the screen. The message says "We'll call it:", and then it adds the value stored in the 'box_name' variable using an f-string. The {box_name} part gets replaced with whatever the user typed in response to the question.

print()

Alright, let's start by addressing why output is so crucial. Imagine you've just written an awesome program that solves complex equations. If you can't see the solutions, how useful is that? Not very, right? That's why output is so crucial—it's like the grand finale of a fireworks show, the moment we've all been waiting for.

In Python, using print() is quite straightforward. This function allows you to output text, numbers, and even more complex data types like lists and dictionaries, directly to the console or terminal. Let's consider a simple example:

```python
# Example 1: Printing a message
print("Hello, World!")

# Example 2: Printing numbers
```

```python
print(42)

# Example 3: Combining text and numbers
age = 30
print("My age is", age)

# Example 4: Printing a list
my_list = [1, 2, 3, 4, 5]
print("The elements in my list are:", my_list)

# Example 5: Printing multiple items using separators
and end parameter
print("This", "is", "Python", sep='-', end='!\n')
```

```
# Output:
Hello, World!
42
My age is 30
The elements in my list are: [1, 2, 3, 4, 5]
This-is-Python!
```

The Basic print()

You've already seen how to use print() for simple messages and numbers, like print("Hello, World!") and print(42). Easy-peasy, isn't it?

Meet the List

Now, let's get a bit more sophisticated. You can also print a list using the print() function. A list is a collection of items, and it's one of Python's most versatile data types.

```
my_list = [1, 2, 3]
print(my_list)
```

When you run this, you'll see [1, 2, 3] printed on your screen. Nothing complicated, right? Just remember that lists are enclosed in square brackets, and the items inside are separated by commas.

'sep' and 'end' Parameters

Now, here's where things get really interesting. The print() function has some optional parameters, like sep and end, that give you more control over your output.

- sep: This stands for "separator" and defines what goes between the items you're printing. The default is a space.

- end: This one's about what gets printed at the very end. The default is a new line, meaning the cursor will move to the next line after printing.

For example:

```
print("This", "is", "Python", sep="-", end="!\n")
```

```
# Output will be: This-is-Python!
```

Here, the sep="-" replaces spaces with hyphens, and end="!\n" adds an exclamation mark followed by a new line.

Syntax, Syntax, Syntax!

While you're getting to grips with all this, don't forget the basics:

- Use commas to separate items within print().
- Be consistent with your quotes—if you start with a double, end with a double.
- When you're dealing with lists, mind your square brackets.

Make a syntax mistake, and Python will give you an error message. But don't worry; even seasoned programmers make these mistakes. The key is to **practice, practice, practice**!

Hold on tight, because our next chapter is going to be even more fascinating! Keep that enthusiasm high and your keyboards ready. We're diving deeper into the world of coding next!

4

Python Operators

We have come to a fascinating topic to dive into: Operators in Python! Now you might be wondering, "Operators? What are those?"

Think of operators as the "doers" in the Python world. They perform specific tasks on variables and values, just like a cable operator provides dish line service to your TV. In Python, operators are tiny but powerful tools that help you manipulate data and make decisions.

Types of Operators in Python

Python offers a variety of operators, and understanding these is key to becoming proficient in the language. Let's break them down into categories:

1. Arithmetic Operators
2. Comparison Operator
3. Logical operators
4. Assignment Operator
5. Membership operators
6. Identity operators
7. Bit-wise operator

1. Arithmetic Operators

Arithmetic operators are used for performing mathematical operations like addition, subtraction, multiplication, and so on.

Operator	Description	Example
+	Addition	a + b
-	Subtraction	a - b
*	Multiplication	a * b
/	Division	a / b
%	Modulus	a % b
**	Exponentiation	a ** b
//	Floor Division	a // b

```
x = 10
y = 5

print(x + y)
```
Output: 15

While most of you are familiar with how addition (+), subtraction (-), and multiplication (*) operators work from basic arithmetic, it's worth noting that in Python, we use the forward slash (/) to perform division. So, when you're dividing numbers, keep an eye out for that / symbol—it's your go-to for all things division-related in Python code.

```
x = 10
y = 3

print(x / y)
```
Output: 3.3333333333333335

Here we calculate the quotient. And we got the quotient in decimal. In real-world scenarios, sometimes you don't want a decimal result when dividing.

For instance, if you have 10 motorbikes to divide among 3 people, you can't really give each person 3.33 motorbikes, right? In such cases, someone will either get one more bike, or there will be a bike left over.

In Python, you can use the floor division operator (//) to handle this. Floor division divides and rounds down to the nearest whole number, giving you a result without any decimals. So in this case, 10 // 3 would give you 3, indicating that each person gets 3 motorbikes and one is left over.

```
x = 10
y = 3

print(x // y)
# Output: 3
```

So, if you execute 10 // 3 in Python, the output will be 3, not 3.33. Why does it round down to 3 instead of rounding up to 4? By default, Python performs "floor" division, which means it rounds down to the nearest whole number.

Don't worry, there are ways to round up, or "ceiling" the division, which we will explore in later lessons.

```
x = 19
y = 5

print(x / y)
print(x // y)
```

```
# Output:
3.8
3
```

Let's talk about the % operator, also known as the modulus operator. While the symbol might remind you of percentages, its role in Python is different. It's actually used to find the remainder when one number is divided by another.

For example, if we divide 11 by 3, the quotient is 3 and the remainder is 2. In Python, the modulus operator helps us find this remainder. When you execute 11 % 3, the output will be 2, which is precisely the remainder in this division operation. So, remember, the % operator is your go-to for finding remainders in Python.

```
x = 11
y = 3

print(x % y)
# Output: 2
```

Let's turn our attention to the double asterisk ** operator. In Python, this operator is used for exponentiation, allowing you to calculate the power of a number. For instance, if you want to find the square of 3, you'd use 3 ** 2, and the result would be 9. So when you're looking to raise a number to a specific power, the ** operator is what you'll use in Python.

```
print(3 ** 2)
```
Output: 9

2. Comparison Operators

These operators are used for comparing values. They return either True or False.

Operator	Description	Example
==	Equal to	a == b
!=	Not equal to	a != b
>	Greater than	a > b
<	Less than	a < b
>=	Greater than or equal to	a >= b
<=	Less than or equal to	a <= b

```
x = 10
y = 5

print(x == y)
```
Output: False

```
x = 10
y = 5

print(x > y)
```
Output: True

```
x = 10
y = 5

print(x >= y)
```
Output: True

3. Logical Operators

Logical operators are used to combine conditional statements.

Operator	Description	Example
and	Logical AND	a and b
or	Logical OR	a or b
not	Logical NOT	not a

and

Imagine you and your friends are planning a trip to the zoo. You've set two conditions for going: the zoo should be less than 10 KM away, and the ticket price should be no more than $5.

In this case, you're dealing with multiple logical conditions that both have to be met for you to join the outing. In programming terms, you'd express this using the and operator:

distance <= 10 and ticket_fare <= 5

Only if both of these conditions are true will you decide to go to the zoo.

One of your friends says the distance is 7 km and the ticket fare is $2. So now both conditions are met, so you will go to the zoo.

```
distance_from_home = 7
ticket_fare = 2

print(distance_from_home < 10 and ticket_fare <= 5)
# Output: True
```

A truth table is a great way to understand how the and operator works. In Python, the and operator takes two Boolean values (True or False) and returns True only if both values are True. Here's the truth table:

Input 1	Input 2	Output (and)
True	True	True

True	False	False
False	True	False
False	False	False

In this table, you can see that the and operator returns True only when both Input 1 and Input 2 are True. For all other combinations, the output is False. We can create the table using 0 and 1, where 0 represents 'False' and 1 represents 'True'.

or

Once you're inside the zoo, one of your friends suggests grabbing something to eat. Another friend chimes in, recommending either ice cream or a cold drink. Everyone seems to agree with this suggestion. You're fine with either option, and you could even go for both.

```
choice = "ice cream"

print(choice == "ice cream" or choice == "cold drinks")
# Output: True
```

```
choice = "ice cream"

print(choice == "Chocolate" or choice == "Coffee")
```

```
# Output: False
```

Here's the truth table:

Input 1	Input 2	Output (or)
True	True	True
True	False	True
False	True	True
False	False	False

In this table, you can see that the or operator returns True when either Input 1 or Input 2 is True. The output is False only when both inputs are False.

not

Is 90 bigger than 100? No, it's not. Python also recognizes this as false.

However, if we say "90 is not bigger than 100," that statement is true, correct? In Python, using the not operator before a false condition flips it to true. Similarly, using not before a true condition makes it false.

So, not True equals False, and not False equals True.

```
print(90 > 100)
```
Output: False

Now, if we want to make this statement true, what can we do? All we have to do is add a 'not' before the statement.

```
print(not 90 > 100)
```
Output: True

The not operator in Python is a unary operator, meaning it only takes one input value. Its function is to invert the value of a Boolean expression: True becomes False, and False becomes True. Here's the truth table for the not operator:

Input 1	Output (not)
True	False
False	True

In this table, you can see that not True returns False, and not False returns True. It's a straightforward way to invert a Boolean value.

4. Assignment Operators

Assignment operators are used to assign values to variables.

Operator	Description	Example
=	Assignment	a = b
+=	Add and assign	a += b
-=	Subtract and assign	a -= b
*=	Multiply and assign	a *= b
/=	Divide and assign	a /= b
%=	Modulus and assign	a %= b
**=	Exponent and assign	a **= b
//=	Floor divide and assign	a //= b

Assignment

You've already seen that we can assign a value to a variable using the = symbol.

```
# Assigning a value '50' into a variable 'a'
a = 50

print(a)
# Output: 50
```

Add and assign

In addition to simply assigning a value to a variable using the = symbol, you can also add and assign a value to a variable using the += operator. This allows you to update the value of a variable by adding a specific amount to it. For example:

```
# Assigning a value 50 into a variable
a = 50
# Adding and assigning 5 more into the variable
a += 5

print(a)
# Output: 55
```

After executing the above code, the new value of a would be 55. The += operator takes the current value of the variable, adds the specified value to it, and then reassigns the new value back to the variable.

Subtract and assign

You can use the -= operator to subtract a value from a variable and update that variable with the new value in a single step. This is known as "subtract and assign.

```
# Assigning a value 50 into a variable
a = 50
# subtracting and assigning the new value into the
```

```
variable
a -= 5

print(a)
```
Output: 45

After executing this code, the new value of y would be 45. The -= operator takes the current value of the variable, subtracts the specified amount from it, and then reassigns the updated value back to the variable.

Multiply and assign

You can use the *= operator to multiply a variable by a specific value and then update the variable with the new value.

```
# Assigning a value 50 into a variable
a = 50
# Multiplying and assigning the new value into the
variable
a *= 5

print(a)
```
Output: 250

Divide and assign

You can use the /= operator for division and assignment in a single step.

```
a = 50
a /= 5

print(a)
# Output: 10.0
```

Modulus and assign

You can use the %= operator to find the remainder of a division operation and update the variable with the new value.

```
a = 50
a %= 5

print(a)
# Output: 0
```

After executing this code, the new value of a would be 0, as 50 divided by 5 leaves a remainder of 0.

Exponent and assign

You can use the **= operator to raise a variable to a specific power and then update the variable with the new value.

```
a = 5
a **= 2

print(a)
# Output: 25
```

After running this code, the new value of a would be 25, because 5 raised to the power of 2 equals 25. The **= operator takes the current value of the variable, raises it to the specified power, and then reassigns the new value back to the variable.

Floor divide and assign

You can use the //= operator to perform floor division on a variable and then update that variable with the new value in a single operation.

```
a = 5
a //= 2

print(a)
# Output: 2
```

After running this code, the new value of d would be 2. This is because 5 divided by 2 is 2.5, and the floor division // rounds down to the nearest whole number, which is 2 in this case.

5. Membership Operators

Imagine you and some friends are planning a trip to the zoo. You're checking to see if everyone is present. Each friend who is already there says, "I'm in," while anyone who isn't there yet says, "I'm not in the group."

The membership operators in Python work in a similar way. Using in checks if a certain value is present in a variable and returns True if it is. On the other hand, using not in checks if a value is absent from a variable, and if it's not there, it returns True.

```python
group = "Avenger"

print("A" in group)
# Output: True
```

In this example, 'A' is present in the word 'Avenger,' which is why the output is True. The same holds true for the other letters 'v,' 'e,' 'n,' 'g,' 'e,' and 'r.'

However, if we use 'a' instead of 'A,' the result will be different.

```python
group = "Avenger"
```

```
print("a" in group)
# Output: False
```

Why is it false? The reason is that Python is case-sensitive, as you already know.

Membership operators test for membership in a sequence such as lists, strings, or tuples.

Operator	Description	Example
in	In	x in y
not in	Not in	x not in y

6. Identity Operators

Identity operators in Python work on a similar principle to how objects occupy space in the real world. Just as everything around you, including the air, takes up space, a music file on your computer also occupies space in its memory.

Just like every object in the real world occupies a unique space, every object in Python has a unique identity, represented by its location in memory. When you use the 'is' operator, you're essentially asking, "Are these two things really the same object occupying the same space in memory?"

```
x = [1, 2, 3]
y = x
z = [1, 2, 3]

print(x is y)
print(x is z)
# Output:
True
False
```

On the flip side, the 'is not' operator checks if two variables point to different objects:

```
x = [1, 2, 3]
y = x
z = [1, 2, 3]

print(x is not y)
print(x is not z)
# Output:
False
True
```

Remember, 'is' and 'is not' are different from '==' and '!='. The '==' operator checks if two variables are equal in value, whereas 'is' checks if they refer to the same object in memory.

So, in summary, identity operators are like asking, "Are these two things the exact same object in memory?" or "Do these two things occupy different spaces in memory?"

Identity operators are used to compare objects.

Operator	Description	Example
is	Identity	a is b
is not	Not Identity	a is not b

Exercises

Arithmetic Operations: Calculate the area of a rectangle using arithmetic operators.

```
# Take user input for the length of the rectangle, for
example, user pressed: 7
length = float(input("Enter the length of the rectangle:
"))

# Take user input for the width of the rectangle, for
example, user pressed: 9
width = float(input("Enter the width of the rectangle:
"))
```

```
# Calculate the area of the rectangle Using the
arithmetic operator '*' for multiplication
area = length * width

# Display the result
print(f"The area of the rectangle with length {length}
and width {width} is {area}.")
```

```
# Output:
The area of the rectangle with length 7.0 and width 8.0
is 56.0.
```

In this example, we used the multiplication operator * to calculate the area. The program takes the length and width as inputs, converts them to floating-point numbers using float() function (so that they can be decimals), and then multiplies them together to get the area, which it then prints out.

Comparison Exercise: Check if the number 25 is odd using comparison operators.

```
# Given number
number = 25

# Check if the number is odd
is_odd = number % 2 == 1  # Using the modulus
operator `%` and the comparison operator `==`
```

```
# Display the result
if is_odd:
    print(f"The number {number} is odd.")
else:
    print(f"The number {number} is not odd.")
```
```
# Output:
The number 25 is odd.
```

In this example, 'number % 2' will be 1 because 25 divided by 2 leaves a remainder of 1. Then we use the comparison operator '==' to check if this remainder is equal to 1. If it is, the number is odd, and the variable 'is_odd' will be True.

So, the program will output "The number 25 is odd."

Logical Test: Create a logical expression that checks if a number is divisible by 2 and 3.

```
# Given number, suppose user entered 30
number = int(input("Enter a number: "))

# Logical expression to check if the number is divisible
by 2 and 3
is_divisible_by_2_and_3 = (number % 2 == 0) and
(number % 3 == 0)
```

```
# Display the result
print(f"The statement that the number {number} is
divisible by 2 and 3 is {is_divisible_by_2_and_3}.")
```

```
# Output:
The statement that the number 30 is divisible by 2 and
3 is True.
```

In this example suppose a user has given 30 as an input here.

30 is divisible by 2: 30 % 2 == 0 evaluates to True

30 is also divisible by 3: 30 % 3 == 0 evaluates to True

Both conditions are met, so the and operator would combine these two True values to produce a final value of True.

Assignment Exercise: Initialize a variable with the value 10, double it using assignment operators, and print the result.

```
# Initialize a variable with the value 10
my_variable = 10

# Double the variable's value using the *= assignment
operator
my_variable *= 2  # This is equivalent to my_variable =
my_variable * 2
```

```
# Print the result
print(f"The doubled value is {my_variable}.")
```

```
# Output:
The doubled value is 20.
```

Here, a variable called 'my_variabl'e is initialized with the value of 10. In Python, the '=' operator is used for assignment, which means the value on the right (10) is stored in the variable on the left ('my_variable').

After that, the '*=' assignment operator is used to double the value of 'my_variable'. The expression 'my_variable *= 2' is a shorthand way of writing 'my_variable = my_variable * 2'.

Membership Test: Check if the letter "y" is in the word "Python".

```
# Given word
word = "Python"

# Check if 'y' is in the word
is_present = 'y' in word

# Print the result
print(f"The   letter   'y'   is   in   the   word   'Python':
```

```
{is_present}")
```

```
# Output:
The letter 'y' is in the word 'Python': True
```

In this example, the variable 'is_present' will hold the value 'True' if the letter 'y' is found in the string stored in 'word', and 'False' otherwise. The 'print()' function then displays this boolean value.

Identity Test: Create two lists with identical elements. Check if they are identical objects.

```
# Create two lists with identical elements
list1 = [1, 2, 3]
list2 = [1, 2, 3]

# Check if they are identical objects using the 'is'
keyword
result = list1 is list2

# Print the result
print("Are list1 and list2 identical objects?", result)
```

```
# Output:
Are list1 and list2 identical objects? False
```

The two lists 'list1' and 'list2' contain the same elements ('[1, 2, 3]'), but they are two distinct objects stored at different memory locations. Therefore, the is operator will return 'False', indicating that they are not identical objects.

In Python, the is operator checks for object identity, meaning it checks whether two variables point to the same object in memory, not whether the objects have the same content.

That's it for this lesson. In the next lesson, we'll delve into control flow statements in Python. Happy coding!

5

Data Types

W hat is a data type? You might be wondering if I'm introducing new terminology again, but don't worry, this is a fairly straightforward concept. You're already familiar with what data is. For instance, your age represents data about you, just like your phone number and address do.

Let's consider a hypothetical scenario: If I ask you for your exam marks and you give me your address, we have a mismatch. Exam marks should be numerical, while addresses are composed of text. This brings us to the concept of data types.

Here's an illustrative example:

Name: John
Age: 30
Phone: 011474747
Height: 5.10
Address: Baker Street, USA

In this example, each piece of information is data, but they belong to different data types.

The name "John" is a type of data called text or string, as it's made up of characters.

The age, 30, is an integer because it's a whole number without any fractional components.

The phone number, while made up of digits, is generally considered a string because you don't perform mathematical operations on it.

The height, 5.10, is what we call a floating-point number because it has a decimal point.

Finally, the address "Baker Street, USA" is another text or string type of data, consisting of a series of characters.

Each of these pieces of information is data, but they each belong to a different data type because they are meant to represent different kinds of information.

Some of the data types are:

- Integer
- Float
- String
- Boolean

What is Integer?

In Python, an integer is a whole number that can be either positive, negative, or zero. Unlike floating-point numbers, integers do not have a decimal point.

For example, the numbers -3, -2, -1, 0, 1, 2, and 3 are all integers. In a Python program, you could assign an integer value to a variable like this:

```
age = 30

print(type(age))
# Output: <class 'int'>
```

In this Python code snippet, there are two lines:

1. age = 30: This line declares a variable named 'age' and assigns the integer value '30' to it. In other words, the

variable 'age' now holds the value '30'..

2. print(type(age)): This line uses the 'print()' function to display the output of 'type(age)'. The 'type()' function is used to find out the data type of a given variable or value. In this case, 'type(age)' will show the output '<class 'int'>', indicating that the variable 'age' is of integer data type.

When you run this code, it will output <class 'int'>, confirming that the variable age is an integer.

What is Float?

In Python, a "float" is a data type used to store floating-point numbers, which are numbers that have a decimal point. For example, the number 5.71 is a floating-point number, and in Python, you would represent it as a float. Here's a simple example:

```
height = 5.71

print(type(height))
# Output: <class 'float'>
```

when you print the output of 'type(height)', it confirms that the data type of 'height' is indeed a float by displaying '<class

'float'>'.

So, the output '<class 'float'>' is telling you that the variable 'height' is storing a floating-point number.

Keep in mind that, you can perform any mathematical operation between integers and floats. For example:

```
a = 103
b = 51.73

print(a+b)
# Output: 154.73
```

What is String?

Letter, word, sentence - these are all strings in Python. Just as numbers are important for calculations and data analysis, words and text are equally crucial for communication and data representation in programs.

To define a string in Python, you simply enclose it in quotation marks. For example, you can use either "hello" or 'hello' to create a string. So, just like you need numbers for certain tasks, you'll need strings to represent and manipulate text.

```
my_text = 'hello!'
my_text_2 = "I am learning python"

print(my_text, my_text_2)
```
```
# Output: hello! I am learning python
```

Do you remember using the 'type()' function to find out the datatype of a variable? Let's apply it in an example to identify a string type.:

```
my_text = 'hello!'

print(type(my_text))
```
```
# Output: <class 'str'>
```

Here, the 'type()' function is used to display the datatype of the variable 'my_text', which contains the string 'hello!'; the output '<class 'str'>' confirms that it is a string.

What happens if we put an integer or float inside quotation marks?

```
my_text = '57'

print(type(my_text))
```

```
<class 'str'>
```

```
my_text = '109.63'

print(type(my_text))
```
```
# Output: <class 'str'>
```

Is it confusing? Look, If you put an integer or float inside quotation marks, Python will treat it as a string.

For example, if you write '57' or '109.63', although they look like numbers, they will be considered strings because they are enclosed in quotes. Therefore, you won't be able to perform mathematical operations on them as you would with actual integers or floats.

Ready for a challenge? Try printing the following sentence: "Do not go outside, it's raining." You might think to write it as print('Do not go outside, it's raining.'), but this will lead to an error. Try it.

```
print('Don not go outside, it's raining.')
```
```
# Output: SyntaxError: invalid syntax.
```

But why? Because the single quotation marks inside the sentence conflict with the ones used to define the string, making Python think the string ends at "it's."

The solution is to use double quotation marks on the outside, like this: print("Do not go outside, it's raining."), or to use single quotes on the inside and double quotes on the outside, and vice versa.

```
print("Do not go outside, it's raining.")
# Output: Do not go outside, it's raining.
```

How 5 + 5 = 55! Math or Magic?

Let me demonstrate a basic math operation for you: simple addition, like 5 + 5, which we all know equals 10. But now, prepare yourself for a little twist.

```
print('5' + '5')
# Output: 55
```

So what's the secret? The trick lies in the quotation marks. Instead of using 5 as an integer, I used it as a string by enclosing it in quotes. This is known as string concatenation, where the '+' operator is used to join strings together.

Let's assign it to a variable and then check the datatype of that variable.

```
a = '5' + '5'

print(type(a))
# Output: <class 'str'>
```

You can see the datatype of the variable is a string.

Let's see another example:

```
a = 'Do not go outside'
b = 'It is raining'

print(a+b)
# Output: Do not go outsideIt is raining
```

But there is no space between 'outside' and 'it', Right? That's because we didn't include a space when we printed the variables 'a' and 'b' together. Let's add a space.

```
a = 'Do not go outside'
b = 'It is raining'

print(a+ ' ' +b)
```

```
# Output: Do not go outside It is raining
```

Here, we inserted a space within quotes because a space is treated as a string. That's why it's enclosed in quotation marks, and we used the '+' operator to concatenate all the elements together.

We can have a little fun by converting all the letters to capitalize, lowercase, or uppercase functions. Let's check out the examples:

```
a = 'He enjoyed a cup of coffee before starting work.'

print(a.upper())
```
```
# Output: HE ENJOYED A CUP OF COFFEE BEFORE
STARTING WORK.
```

upper(): This function converts all the characters in a string to uppercase.

```
a = 'He enjoyed a cup of coffee before starting work.'

print(a.lower())
```
```
# Output: he enjoyed a cup of coffee before starting
work.
```

lower(): This function turns all the characters in a string to lowercase.

```
a = 'he enjoyed a cup of coffee before starting work.'

print(a.capitalize())
```
```
# Output:
He enjoyed a cup of coffee before starting work.
```

capitalize(): This function capitalizes only the first character of the string while making the rest lowercase.

```
a = 'he enjoyed a cup of coffee before starting work.'

print(a.title())
```
```
# Output:
He Enjoyed A Cup Of Coffee Before Starting Work.
```

title(): This function capitalizes the first letter of each word in the string, turning all other characters to lowercase.

The Friendship of Einstein, Newton, and Curie - split() and join()

Einstein, Newton, and Curie are in a classroom, more focused on planning a hangout than on their studies. Recognizing this, the teacher decides they should be separated to prevent further distraction.

To do this, the teacher employs the split() function to divide them up.

```
a = 'Einstein Newton Curie'

print(a.split())
# Output:
['Einstein', 'Newton', 'Curie']
```

In this example, 'a' = 'Einstein Newton Curie' is a single string containing the names of the three scientists. When we use 'a.split()', it breaks the single string into a list of individual strings, separating them based on spaces. So the output would be '['Einstein', 'Newton', 'Curie']'.

Now, they are still in the same class but separated into individual strings. If the teacher changes their mind and wants to put them back together, the 'join()' function can be used. This will concatenate the individual strings back into a single string, effectively putting Einstein, Newton, and Curie back together. In this way, the three names become a single string again.

```
a = ['Einstein', 'Newton', 'Curie']

print(' '.join(a))
# Output: Einstein Newton Curie
```

The 'join()' function operates a bit differently than you might expect. You have to specify what will go between the elements that are being joined. In the earlier example, we used a space as the separator. To clarify, let's look at a few examples:

```
# Using a comma and a space
a = ['Einstein', 'Newton', 'Curie']

print(', '.join(a))
```
```
# Output:
Einstein, Newton, Curie
```

```
# Using a hyphen
a = ['Einstein', 'Newton', 'Curie']

print('-'.join(a))
```
```
# Output:
Einstein-Newton-Curie
```

Measuring with len()

Curious about the length of a string? The len() function in Python can provide that information for you.

```
string = 'cat'

print(len(string))
```
```
# Output:
3
```

Let's see another example:

```
string = 'There is a dog'

print(len(string))
```
```
# Output:
14
```

Let's make it clear

T	h	e	r	e		i	s		a		d	o	g
0	1	2	3	4	5	6	7	8	9	10	11	12	13

So, 5 (from 'There') + 2 (from 'is') + 1 (from 'a') + 3 (from 'dog') + 3 (spaces) = 14 characters in total. So, Python is counting the spaces too.

From this string, we can access any character based on its index position. For example, the character at index 0 is 'T', and the character at index 11 is 'd'.

```
string = 'There is a dog'

print(string[11])
```
```
# Output:
d
```

If we say to print from index 0 to index 7:

```
string = 'There is a dog'

print(string[0:7])
```
```
# Output:
There i
```

In this case, you'll notice that the letter 's' is not included in the output though it is the 7th index. That's because Python prints up to one index before the upper limit specified. But the lower limit works as usual.

If we provide only the start index and omit the end index, Python will assume we want to go all the way to the end of the string.

```
string = 'There is a dog'

print(string[7:])
```
```
# Output:
```

```
s a dog
```

Similarly, if we don't specify either a start or an end index, Python will output the entire string.

```
string = 'There is a dog'

print(string[:])
```
```
# Output:
There is a dog
```

Boolean - True or false:

Consider this as a specialized form of integer where True equates to 1 and False to 0. Booleans are particularly useful when you need a binary answer, either True or False.

```
is_raining = False
print(type(is_raining))
```
```
# Output:
<class 'bool'>
```

In the example, we declare a variable named 'is_raining' and assign it the value 'False'. The 'type()' function is then used to determine the datatype of this variable. When we print it out, the output shows '<class 'bool'>', confirming that 'is_raining' is indeed a Boolean variable. Don't worry if you're still curious about how to use Booleans; we'll explore their usage in greater detail later on.

Type Casting -Change one data type into another

We've already explored various data types such as integers, floats, strings, and Booleans. Fortunately, Python allows us to convert one data type to another as needed.

To perform these conversions, we can make use of built-in functions like int(), float(), and str().

int()

The int() function in Python is used to convert a value into an integer. This can be particularly useful when you have a number in a different data type, such as a float or a string, and you want to change it to an integer.

Let's go through some examples:

Converting a float to an integer:

```
float_data = 5.7
```

```
integer_data = int(float_data)

print(integer_data)
```
```
# Output:
5
```

Here, the 'int()' function rounds down the float '5.7' to the integer '5'.

Converting a string to an integer:

```
my_string = "42"
my_integer = int(my_string)

print(type(my_integer))
```
```
# Output:
<class 'int'>
```

Here we can see the datatype changes to integer, And the value must be 42.

Converting a boolean to an integer:

```
my_bool = True
my_integer = int(my_bool)
```

```
print(my_integer)
```

```
# Output:
1
```

Here, True is converted to the integer 1, as in Boolean logic, True is equivalent to 1.

It's important to note that the value you are trying to convert should be convertible to an integer. For example, you can't convert the string "hello" to an integer because it doesn't represent a numerical value.

str()

The str() function in Python serves to convert a given value into a string. This is especially useful when you have data in other types, such as integers, floats, or Booleans, and you want to convert them to string format for tasks like text manipulation or printing.

Here are some illustrative examples:

Converting an integer to a string:

```
my_integer = 10
my_string = str(my_integer)
```

```
print(type(my_string))
```

```
# Output:
<class 'str'>
```

In this example, the integer 10 is converted to the string. Now we can't do any numerical calculation with this.

Converting a Boolean to a string:

```
my_bool = False
my_string = str(my_bool)

print(my_string)
```

```
# Output:
False
```

6

D a t a   S t r u c t u r e s

We have already talked about putting a value, or data, into something called a 'variable,' right? Imagine you have a bunch of different fruits like apple, banana, and orange. You want to store each fruit in a basket like...

```
basket_1 = 'Apple'
basket_2 = 'Banana'
basket_3 = 'Orange'
```

What do you think about this approach? If we use a separate basket for each type of fruit, it could take up a lot of space, couldn't it?

What if we put all the different fruits into just one basket? To give you an example, let's say we have a single basket and we call it 'basket_of_fruits.' We can then put all our different fruits right into that one basket.

```
basket_of_fruits = ['Apple', 'Banana', 'Orange']
```

In the example basket_of_fruits = ['Apple', 'Banana', 'Orange'], we're using Python programming to create a list. This list is like a single basket that's holding three different fruits: Apple, Banana, and Orange.

- 'basket_of_fruits' is the name of the list, or you could say it's the label on our 'basket.'
- The equal sign '=' is used for assignment. This tells Python to put the fruits into the basket.
- '['Apple', 'Banana', 'Orange']' is the actual list. Each fruit is a string (text data), and they're separated by commas. The square brackets [ ] indicate the beginning and end of the list.

So, 'basket_of_fruits' is now a single, organized place where you're storing the names of three different fruits. You can easily add more fruits, take some out, or even rearrange them if you want to!

Think of data structures as a way to hold similar types of data in an organized manner. Just like you'd group fruits in a basket, you can use a data structure to group related data together in your program.

list()

We have already seen how to make list, we give it a name then put square braces to hold the data separated by comma, here each data is called element/item.

Alright, so we've learned how to create a list. A list is really versatile; you can do a lot with it because it's a "mutable" data structure. What does mutable mean? It means you can change it! You can add fruits, remove them, or update the list as you like.

Going back to our 'basket_of_fruits' example with three types of fruit, we can do numbering them like this...

basket_of_fruits = ['Apple', 'Banana', 'Orange']		
0	1	2

You might wonder, "Why start counting from 0?" Well, in programming, we usually start counting from 0, a concept known as indexing.

So if I ask you, "What fruit is at index 2?" you'll see it's an orange. How would we find this out using Python?

```
basket_of_fruits = ['Apple', 'Banana', 'Orange']

print(basket_of_fruits[2])
# Output:
Orange
```

In the first line we have created a list named 'basket_of_fruits' with three fruits. Then we ask it to print the fruit at index '2'. Because indexing starts from 0 in programming, the fruit at index 2 is 'Orange'. Therefore, the output will be "Orange."

You can also grab a value from the list using its index number, store it in a new variable, and then print that variable. Here's how you can do it:

```
basket_of_fruits = ['Apple', 'Banana', 'Orange']
value = basket_of_fruits[2]

print(value)
# Output:
```

Orange

What we've learned here is about counting from 0 upwards—0, 1, 2, and so on. This is known as forward indexing. There's also something called backward indexing, which starts from -1 and goes to -2, -3, -4, and so forth. Take a look at the number line below to see how it works.

basket_of_fruits = ['Apple', 'Banana', 'Orange']		
-3	-2	-1

```
basket_of_fruits = ['Apple', 'Banana', 'Orange']
value = basket_of_fruits[-2]

print(value)
```
| # Output: |
| Banana |

We know our list has three items, but what if it had many more? Counting manually might not always be practical.

Fortunately, Python can do this easily for us with the len() function, which tells us the number of items in the list.

```
basket_of_fruits = ['Apple', 'Banana', 'Orange']
value = len(basket_of_fruits)

print(value)
```
```
# Output:
3
```

Add item/element to the list

We have three ways to add items to a list in Python: 'append()', 'insert()', and 'extend()'. Let's take a closer look at each method.

append()

To add an item to a list, we can use the 'append()' method. It adds the item to the end of the list.

```
basket_of_fruits = ['Apple', 'Banana', 'Orange']
basket_of_fruits.append('Pineapple')

print(basket_of_fruits)
```
```
# Output:
['Apple', 'Banana', 'Orange', 'Pineapple']
```

In this example the 'append()' method is used to add the item 'Pineapple' to the end of the existing 'basket_of_fruits' list. After this operation, the list will contain four fruits, with 'Pineapple' being the last one.

insert()

In the example above, we added 'Pineapple' to the end of the list. But what if we want to place 'Pineapple' right after 'Banana'? For this, we can use the 'insert()' method. Here's how it works:

```
basket_of_fruits = ['Apple', 'Banana', 'Orange']
basket_of_fruits.insert(2, 'Pineapple')

print(basket_of_fruits)
# Output:
['Apple', 'Banana', 'Pineapple', 'Orange']
```

Here, 'basket_of_fruits.insert(2, 'Pineapple')' uses the 'insert()' method to add 'Pineapple' at the index '2' of the 'basket_of_fruits' list. This means that 'Pineapple' will be placed right after 'Banana' (which is at index 1), pushing 'Orange' (formerly at index 2) to index 3.

['Apple', 'Banana', 'Pineapple', 'Orange']			
0	1	2	3

So, after this operation, the list becomes ['Apple', 'Banana', 'Pineapple', 'Orange'], with 'Pineapple' inserted at the specified index.

extend()

To combine two lists, you can use the extend() method. Lets see an example:

```
basket_of_fruits = ['Apple', 'Banana', 'Orange']
basket_of_fruits_2 = ['Grape', 'Strawberry', 'Pear']
basket_of_fruits.extend(basket_of_fruits_2)

print(basket_of_fruits)
# Output:
['Apple', 'Banana', 'Orange', 'Grape', 'Strawberry',
'Pear']
```

Here, 'basket_of_fruits.extend(basket_of_fruits_2)' uses the 'extend()' method to add all the items from the 'basket_of_fruits_2' list to the end of the 'basket_of_fruits' list. As a result, the original 'basket_of_fruits' list is updated to include the additional fruits ('Grape', 'Strawberry', 'Pear') at the end. After this operation, the combined list is '['Apple', 'Banana', 'Orange', 'Grape', 'Strawberry', 'Pear']'

Updating list

Now we know how to add elements to a list. But, what if we want to update one?

First, we need to identify the index of the item we want to

change. Then we can assign a new value to that index. For example, let's say we want to update 'Orange'.

```
basket_of_fruits = ['Apple', 'Banana', 'Orange', 'Grape',
'Strawberry', 'Pear']
basket_of_fruits[2] = 'Cherry'

print(basket_of_fruits)
# Output:
['Apple', 'Banana', 'Cherry', 'Grape', 'Strawberry',
'Pear']
```

In this code, the line 'basket_of_fruits[2] = 'Cherry'' is where the update happens. It targets the item at index '2' in the 'basket_of_fruits' list, which was originally 'Orange', and replaces it with 'Cherry'.

After this operation, the list becomes '['Apple', 'Banana', 'Cherry', 'Grape', 'Strawberry', 'Pear']', with 'Cherry' taking the place of 'Orange'.

Deleting/removing from list

To remove an item from a list, we can use the pop() method, which deletes the last item of a list. Here's an example:

```
basket_of_fruits = ['Apple', 'Banana',
'Orange', 'Grape', 'Strawberry', 'Pear']
basket_of_fruits.pop()

print(basket_of_fruits)
```

Output:
['Apple', 'Banana', 'Orange', 'Grape', 'Strawberry']

In this example you can see that the last item was 'Pear'. After executing pop(), 'Pear' is removed, and the updated list becomes ['Apple', 'Banana', 'Orange', 'Grape', 'Strawberry'].

However, if we specify an index number when using the pop() method, it will remove the item at that particular index.

```
basket_of_fruits = ['Apple', 'Banana', 'Orange', 'Grape',
'Strawberry', 'Pear']
basket_of_fruits.pop(2)

print(basket_of_fruits)
```

Output:
['Apple', 'Banana', 'Grape', 'Strawberry', 'Pear']

Here we use the 'pop()' method to remove the item at index '2' of the 'basket_of_fruits' list, which is 'Orange'. After this operation, the list updates to ['Apple', 'Banana', 'Grape', 'Strawberry', 'Pear'], with 'Orange' removed.

You can also use the del keyword to remove a specific item from the list. The following example will make it clear:

```
basket_of_fruits = ['Apple', 'Banana', 'Orange', 'Grape',
'Strawberry', 'Pear']
del basket_of_fruits[2]

print(basket_of_fruits)
```
```
# Output:
['Apple', 'Banana', 'Grape', 'Strawberry', 'Pear']
```

You can also eliminate the entire list using the del keyword, effectively removing any trace of its existence.

```
basket_of_fruits = ['Apple', 'Banana', 'Orange', 'Grape',
'Strawberry', 'Pear']
del basket_of_fruits

print(basket_of_fruits)
```
```
# Output:
NameError: name 'basket_of_fruits' is not defined
```

Delete by the value - remove()

To remove an item based on its value, we can use the remove() method. Check out the following code for an example:

```
basket_of_fruits  =  ['Apple',  'Banana',  'Grape',
'Strawberry', 'Pear']
basket_of_fruits.remove('Grape')

print(basket_of_fruits)
```
```
# Output:
['Apple', 'Banana', 'Strawberry', 'Pear']
```

Delete all items at once:

We've seen that the del keyword can remove the entire list. However, if we just want to empty the list of its items while keeping the list itself, we can use the clear() method.

```
basket_of_fruits  =  ['Apple',  'Banana',  'Grape',
'Strawberry', 'Pear']
basket_of_fruits.clear()

print(basket_of_fruits)
```
```
# Output:
[]
```

tuple()

Now, let's talk about tuples. Unlike lists, a tuple is a type of data structure which is immutable; once you create it, you can't change its content. You define a tuple using parentheses '()'. Because of their immutability, tuples are often used for data that shouldn't be altered.

For instance, if you have geographical coordinates for a place, it makes sense to store them in a tuple so they remain constant and aren't accidentally modified.

```
coordinates = (40.7128, -74.0060)

print(type(coordinates))
# Output:
<class 'tuple'>
```

Fun fact: Even if you don't use parentheses, Python will still recognize the values as a tuple if they are separated by commas.

```
coordinates = 40.7128, -74.0060

print(type(coordinates))
# Output:
<class 'tuple'>
```

Access the items

Next, let's explore whether we can modify a tuple. But first, we'll access its values by index in the same way we did with a list.

```
numbers = 'One', 'Two', 'Three', 'Four'

print(numbers[2])
```
```
# Output:
Three
```

Add items to a tuple

Now let's try to add a value to the tuple:

```
numbers = 'One', 'Two', 'Three', 'Four'
numbers[2] = 'five'

print(numbers)
```
```
# Output:
TypeError: 'tuple' object does not support item
assignment
```

As you can see, we can't add or delete items from an existing tuple (will get an error like the example above). However, we can create a new tuple by concatenating two existing ones. Check out the example to see how it's done.

```
numbers = ('One', 'Two', 'Three', 'Four')
numbers_2 = ('Five', 'Six')

print(numbers+numbers_2)
```

Output:
('One', 'Two', 'Three', 'Four', 'Five', 'Six')

Delete

While we can't remove individual items from a tuple, we can delete the entire tuple itself. In other words, you can eliminate the tuple, but you can't alter its contents.

```
numbers = ('One', 'Two', 'Three', 'Four')
del numbers

print(numbers)
```

Output:
NameError: name 'numbers' is not defined

We encountered an error because the tuple 'numbers' no longer exists.

set()

In Python, a set is a data structure that stores unordered, unique items. It's similar to a list or a tuple in some ways, but it comes with its own set of characteristics that make it distinct.

Key Features of Sets:

- Unordered: Sets don't have a specific order. This means you can't index or slice them like you can with lists or tuples.

- Unique Items: Sets only allow unique items, so any duplicate entries are automatically removed.

- Mutable: You can add or remove items from a set after it has been created. However, the items inside a set must be immutable (like integers, floats, strings, and tuples).

Syntax:

You can create a set using curly brackets '{}' or by using the 'set()' constructor.

```
set = {1, 2, 3, 4, 5}

print(type(set))
# Output:
<class 'set'>
```

Here you can see the type '<class 'set'>' is showing as an output.

```
xyz = set([1, 2, 3, 4, 5])

print(type(xyz))
```
```
# Output:
<class 'set'>
```

Here, into the 'set()' function we have given a list using '[ ]' braces. The 'set()' functions contverts it into set type.

The 'print(type(xyz))' line prints the type of the variable 'xyz', which will output '<class 'set'>'. This confirms that 'xyz' is indeed a set data type in Python.

Set holds only unique items

You already know Sets only allow unique items. Let's check it:

```
set = {1, 2, 3, 4, 4, 5}

print(set)
```
```
# Output:
{1, 2, 3, 4, 5}
```

As you can see, when you execute 'print(set)', the output will display the unique elements of the 'set', which is '{1, 2, 3, 4, 5}'. The duplicate '4' is removed.

Indexing:

First off, sets do not support indexing, unlike lists and tuples.

If you try to access an element in a set using an index, Python will throw an error. This is because sets are unordered collections, so the concept of an "index" doesn't apply here. In other words, sets don't remember the sequence of elements.

Adding Elements:

To add a single element to a set, you use the add() method. Here's how it works:

```
my_set = {1, 2, 3, 4, 5}
my_set.add(-7)

print(my_set)
```
```
# Output:
{1, 2, 3, 4, 5, -7}
```

Updating Elements:

By using add() method you can only one item at a time.
But, If you want to add multiple elements at once, you can use the update() method and pass an iterable like a list, tuple, or another set.

```
my_set = {1, 2, 3, 4, 5}
```

```
my_set.update([11, 50, 72])

print(my_set)
```
```
# Output:
{1, 2, 3, 4, 5, 50, 72, 11}
```

Remember that both 'add()' and 'update()' add elements "randomly" because sets are unordered. In lists or tuples, new elements get added to the end, but in sets, there's no such concept.

Deleting Elements:

You can remove an element from a set using the pop(), 'remove()' or the 'discard()' method. The difference is that 'remove()' will raise an error if the element doesn't exist, while 'discard()' won't. 'pop()' always delete elements randomly as set has no index.

```
my_set = {6, 5, 4, 3, 2}
new_set = my_set.pop()

print(new_set)
```
```
# Output:
2
```

```
my_set = {6, 5, 4, 3, 2}
my_set.remove(3)

print(my_set)

# Output will be
```

```
# Output:
{2, 4, 5, 6}
```

```
my_set = {6, 5, 4, 3, 2}
my_set.discard(7)

print(my_set)
```

```
# Output:
{2, 3, 4, 5, 6}
```

Now we will see three fundamental operations you can perform with sets in Python: Union and Intersection and set difference.

These operations come in really handy when you're working with collections of items and want to find commonalities or combine them.

Union

The union operation combines all the unique elements from two or more sets. Think of it as gathering all elements from all involved sets and then removing any duplicates. You can perform union using the union() method or the | operator.

Using union() method:

```
set1 = {1, 2, 3}
set2 = {3, 4, 5}

union_set = set1.union(set2)

print(union_set)
# Output:
{1, 2, 3, 4, 5}
```

Using | operator:

```
set1 = {1, 2, 3}
set2 = {3, 4, 5}

union_set = set1 | set2

print(union_set)
# Output:
{1, 2, 3, 4, 5}
```

Intersection

The intersection operation retrieves all the elements that are common to all the involved sets. It's like finding the shared items between two or more sets. You can use the intersection() method or the & operator for this.

Using intersection() method:

```
set1 = {1, 2, 3}
set2 = {3, 4, 5}

intersection_set = set1.intersection(set2)

print(intersection_set)
# Output:
{3}
```

Using & operator:

```
set1 = {1, 2, 3}
set2 = {3, 4, 5}

intersection_set = set1 & set2

print(intersection_set)

# Output will be:
# Output:
{3}
```

Set Difference

set difference helps you find elements that are in one set but not in another. For example, if you have 'set1 = {1, 2, 3}' and 'set2 = {3, 4, 5}', doing 'set1 - set2' will give you '{1, 2}'. These are the elements present in 'set1' but not in 'set2'. You can also use the 'difference()' method like 'set1.difference(set2)' to get the same result.

```
set1 = {1, 2, 3}
set2 = {3, 4, 5}

difference_set = set1 - set2

print(difference_set)
# Output:
{1, 2}
```

Dictionary - dict()

You already know about dictionary, I am sure you have used it also.Imagine a dictionary as a sort of "lookup table," where you can quickly find information if you know a specific keyword.

In Python, a dictionary (dict) data structure allows you to store key-value pairs, making it easier to organize and retrieve data.

```
my_dict = {'name': 'David Baker',
    'age': 30,
    'email': 'dave@email.com'}


print(my_dict['name'])
```

```
# Output:
David Baker
```

In this example, 'name', 'age', and 'email' are keys, and 'David Baker', '30', and 'dave@email.com' are their respective values. You access values in a dictionary by referring to their key.

Now, let's cover some basic operations you can perform with dictionaries:

Adding or Updating Items

To add a new key-value pair or update an existing one, you can simply assign a value to a key like this:

Add

```
my_dict = {'name': 'David Baker',
    'age': 30,
    'email': 'dave@email.com'}

my_dict['address'] = '123 Street Name'

print(my_dict['address'])
```

```
123 Street Name
```

Update

```
my_dict = {'name': 'David Baker',
      'age': 30,
      'email': 'dave@email.com'}


my_dict['age'] = 42


print(my_dict['age'])
```
```
# Output:
42
```

Delete

To delete an item, you can use the 'del' keyword followed by the key:

```
my_dict = {'name': 'David Baker',
      'age': 30,
      'email': 'dave@email.com'}

del my_dict['age']

print(my_dict['age'])
```
```
# Output:
```

```
KeyError: 'age'
```

Getting All Keys and Values

You can get a list-like object of all keys or values using keys() and values() methods respectively:

```
my_dict = {'name': 'David Baker',
    'age': 30,
    'email': 'dave@email.com'}

all_keys = my_dict.keys()
all_values = my_dict.values()

print(all_keys)
print(all_values)
```

```
# Output:
dict_keys(['name', 'age', 'email'])
dict_values(['David Baker', 30, 'dave@email.com'])
```

List vs Tuple vs Set vs Dict Comparison

Type	Ordered	Mutable	Duplicates	Indexing
List	Yes	Yes	Yes	Yes
Tuple	Yes	No	Yes	Yes

Set	No	Yes	No	No
Dict	Yes (Python 3.7+)	Yes	No (Keys)	Yes (Keys)

Some Common Operations of list-tuple-dictionary

len()

For a list, 'len()' will give you the number of elements in the list.

```
my_list = [1, 2, 3, 4, 5]
length_of_list = len(my_list)


print("Length of list:", length_of_list)
```
```
# Output:
Length of list: 5
```

Similarly, for a tuple, 'len()' returns the number of elements.

```
my_tuple = (1, 2, 3, 4, 5)
length_of_tuple = len(my_tuple)
```

```
print("Length of tuple:", length_of_tuple)
```

```
# Output:
Length of tuple: 5
```

For a set, 'len()' will return the number of unique elements in the set.

```
my_set = {1, 2, 3, 4, 5}
length_of_set = len(my_set)

print("Length of set:", length_of_set)
```

```
# Output:
Length of set: 5
```

In the case of dictionaries, len() returns the number of key-value pairs.

```
my_dict = {'name': 'Dave',
      'age': 35,
      'email': 'alice@email.com',
      'address': 'ABC street, USA',
      'phone': '123456789'}
length_of_dict = len(my_dict)

print("Length of dictionary:", length_of_dict)
```

```
# Output:
```

Length of dictionary: 5

Maximum and minimum element - max(), min()

For a list, 'max()' and 'min()' will give you the largest and smallest elements, respectively.

```python
my_list = [1, 2, 3, 4, 5]

max_list = max(my_list)
min_list = min(my_list)

print("Max in list:", max_list)  # Output will be 5
print("Min in list:", min_list)  # Output will be 1
```

```
# Output:
Max in list: 5
Min in list: 1
```

Similarly, for a tuple, 'max()' and 'min()' will give you the largest and smallest elements.

```python
my_tuple = (1, 2, 3, 4, 5)

max_tuple = max(my_tuple)
min_tuple = min(my_tuple)
```

```
print("Max in tuple:", max_tuple)  # Output will be 5
print("Min in tuple:", min_tuple)  # Output will be 1
```

```
# Output:
Max in tuple: 5
Min in tuple: 1
```

For a set, 'max()' and 'min()' also give you the largest and smallest unique elements.

```
my_set = {1, 2, 3, 4, 5}

max_set = max(my_set)
min_set = min(my_set)

print("Max in set:", max_set)
print("Min in set:", min_set)
```

```
# Output:
Max in set: 5
Min in set: 1
```

For dictionaries, you can find the maximum or minimum among the keys or the values (numbers).

```
my_dict = {'first': 10,
```

```
    'second': 30,
    'third': 20}


max_value = max(my_dict.values())
min_value = min(my_dict.values())


print("Max value in dictionary:", max_value)
print("Min value in dictionary:", min_value)
```

```
# Output:
Max value in dictionary: 30
Min value in dictionary: 10
```

Membership

Checking for membership, or whether a particular element is present in a data structure, is a common task. In Python, you can use the in keyword for this. Let's look at how it works for lists, tuples, sets, and dictionaries.

For lists, the 'in' keyword checks if a certain value is present among the list elements.

```
my_list = [1, 2, 3, 4, 5]
is_present = 3 in my_list


print("Is 3 in the list?", is_present)
```

```
Is 3 in the list? True
```

Similarly, for tuples, the 'in' keyword checks for element presence.

```
my_tuple = (1, 2, 3, 4, 5)
is_present = 6 in my_tuple

print("Is 6 in the tuple?", is_present)
```
```
# Output:
Is 6 in the tuple? False
```

For sets, the 'in' keyword will check if a certain element exists.

```
my_set = {1, 2, 3, 4, 5}
is_present = 2 in my_set

print("Is 2 in the set?", is_present)
```
```
# Output:
Is 2 in the set? True
```

In the case of dictionaries, the 'in' keyword checks if a certain key exists. It does not check for values.

```
my_dict = {'name': 'Alice', 'age': 30, 'email':
```

```
'alice@email.com'}

is_present = 'age' in my_dict

print("Is 'age' a key in the dictionary?", is_present)
```
```
# Output:
Is 'age' a key in the dictionary? True
```

Nested

In programming, "nested" usually means that one data structure is stored inside another. It's like Russian dolls, where each doll contains another smaller one inside.

In Python, you can have nested lists, nested tuples, nested dictionaries, or even combinations like a list inside a tuple or a tuple inside a list. Let's break it down:

Nested Lists

A list within another list is known as a nested list. It's useful when you want to create something like a matrix or a multi-dimensional array.

```
nested_list = [[1, 2, 3], [4, 5, 6], [7, 8, 9]]
```

In our main list, we have three sub-lists. If we were to apply indexing to the main list, it would go like this:

[[1, 2, 3],	[4, 5, 6],	[7, 8, 9]]
0	1	2

If we want to see the output of index 1:

```
nested_list = [[1, 2, 3], [4, 5, 6], [7, 8, 9]]

print(nested_list[1])
```

```
# Output:
[4, 5, 6]
```

We've already seen how to index the main list, but if we want to access items within the sub-lists, the indexing would work like this:

[[1, 2, 3],			[4, 5, 6],			[7, 8, 9]]		
0	1	2	3	4	5	6	7	8
0			1			2		

```
nested_list = [[1, 2, 3], [4, 5, 6], [7, 8, 9]]
```

```
print(nested_list[1][2])
```

```
# Output:
6
```

In this example, nested_list is a list containing three sub-lists. The code aims to access an element from one of these sub-lists.

The line print(nested_list[1][2]) is doing two things:

- nested_list[1]: This part accesses the second sub-list ([4, 5, 6]) in the nested_list. Remember, indexing starts from 0, so [1] gets us the second sub-list.

- [2]: This part is indexing that second sub-list, [4, 5, 6], to get its third element. Again, since indexing starts from 0, [2] gets us the element 6.

So when you combine them, nested_list[1][2] first goes to the second sub-list and then fetches the third element from that sub-list, which is 6. Therefore, the output of the code will be 6.

Using a similar approach, you can also access elements in a nested tuple.

```
nested_tuple = ((1, 2, 3), (4, 5, 6), (7, 8, 9))

print(nested_tuple[1][2])
# Output:
6
```

Mixed Nesting

You can mix data structures, too. For instance, you could have a list within a tuple or a tuple within a list.

```
mixed = [(1, 2, 3), [4, 5, 6], (7, 8, 9)]

print(mixed[1][2])
# Output:
6
```

Nested Dictionaries

Dictionaries can also be nested within dictionaries, or even within lists and tuples. The syntax will be 'value = outer_dict['outer_key']['inner_key']'

```
nested_dict = {
    'person1': {'name': 'Dave', 'age': 32},
    'person2': {'name': 'Tyla', 'age': 35}
```

```
}

result = nested_dict['person1']['name']

print(result)
```
```
# Output:
Dave
```

Here's how the code works:

- nested_dict['person1']: This part accesses the dictionary corresponding to the key 'person1', which is '{'name': 'Dave', 'age': 32}'.

- ['name']: After accessing the inner dictionary, this part fetches the value associated with the key 'name', which is 'Dave'.

The line 'result = nested_dict['person1']['name']' combines these two steps. It first navigates to the dictionary for 'person1' and then fetches the value for the key 'name', which is 'Dave'.

7

C o n d i t i o n s

I n our real life we make decisions based on specific factors or conditions.

let's consider the daily routine of deciding what to wear based on the weather. You wake up in the morning and the first thing you do is check the weather forecast on your phone. If it's going to be a hot and sunny day, you'll likely opt for light clothing like a t-shirt and shorts to stay comfortable.

However, if the forecast indicates rain, your choice naturally shifts to wearing something water-resistant, and you'll probably carry an umbrella as well.

On colder days, a sweater or a jacket becomes the preferred option to keep warm.

When the weather is unpredictable, layering your clothes might be the best approach, so you can adjust as the day progresses.

This way, your decision on what to wear isn't random but is influenced by the information you have about the weather.

See the demonstration below:

If (sunny):

Wear shorts

Or If (rainy):

Carry umbrella

or

Prepare for anything

Similarly, In Python, the syntax for conditional statements, which facilitate decision-making in the code, is structured as follows:

if, elif, and else

```
if condition_1:
```

```
    # code to execute if condition_1 is True
elif condition_2:
    # code to execute if condition_2 is True
else:
    # code to execute if none of the above conditions are
True
```

Let's consider a real-life scenario where you're deciding what to eat for dinner based on how much time you have:

```
# Assign time available to a variable
time_available = 90

# Decision-making based on time available
if time_available >= 60:
    dinner_choice = 'Cook a three-course meal'
elif time_available >= 30:
    dinner_choice = 'Make a quick pasta dish'
else:
    dinner_choice = 'Order takeout'

# Display the dinner choice
print(f"Based on the time you have, you should:
{dinner_choice}")

# Output:
Based on the time you have, you should: Cook a three-
```

course meal

In this example, 'time_available' represents the amount of time you have to prepare dinner. If you have 60 minutes or more, you decide to cook a three-course meal. If you have at least 30 minutes but less than 60, you opt for a quicker option like making pasta. If you have less than 30 minutes, you decide to order takeout.

I am sure you remember the input() function. Here's how you could modify the previous example to ask the user how much time they have available for dinner preparation:

```
# Get user input for time available
time_available = int(input("How many minutes do you have to prepare dinner? "))

# Decision-making based on time available
if time_available >= 60:
    dinner_choice = 'Cook a three-course meal'
elif time_available >= 30:
    dinner_choice = 'Make a quick pasta dish'
else:
    dinner_choice = 'Order takeout'

# Display the dinner choice
```

```
print(f"Based on the time you have, you should:
{dinner_choice}")
```

How Conditions Work in Python

In programming languages, conditions are evaluated as either true or false. If a condition is true, then the code block associated with that condition is executed. On the other hand, if the condition is false, the program skips over that block of code and proceeds to evaluate the next condition, if there is one.

For example, in an 'if-elif-else' structure, the program will check the 'if' condition first. If it's true, it will execute that block of code; if not, it will move on to the 'elif' condition, and so on.

```
is_morning = True
is_afternoon = False
is_evening = False

# Check conditions
if is_morning:
    print("Good morning!")
elif is_afternoon:
    print("Good afternoon!")
else:
```

```
    print("Good evening!")
```

```
# Output:
Good morning!
```

In this example:

The variable 'is_morning' is set to 'True', so the first 'if' condition evaluates to 'true' and "Good morning!" is printed.

Since 'is_morning' is 'true', the program doesn't even check the 'elif' or 'else' blocks; it skips them entirely.

This exemplifies how the boolean values 'True' and 'False' govern the flow of conditional statements. If the first condition (is_morning) were set to 'False' and the second (is_afternoon) were set to 'True', the program would skip the first block and print "Good afternoon!" instead.

```
# Set some boolean conditions
is_morning = False
is_afternoon = True
is_evening = False

# Check conditions
if is_morning:
    print("Good morning!")
elif is_afternoon:
    print("Good afternoon!")
```

```
else:
    print("Good evening!")
```

Output:
Good afternoon!

You might observe that we usually don't insert the literal values 'True' or 'False' directly into conditions. You're correct in noting this. However, as I mentioned earlier, conditions themselves are expressions that evaluate to either true or false.

For example, a condition like 'age >= 60' will produce a 'True' or 'False' result. Based on this evaluation, the program then decides which block of code to execute or skip. So while True or False may not be explicitly written in the condition, the condition is indeed generating a true or false outcome that directs the program's flow.

```
light_color = 'yellow'  # the current color of the traffic light

# Decision based on the color of the light
if light_color == 'green': #The light color is not green, it is false
    action = 'Go'
elif light_color == 'yellow': #The light color is not green,
```

```
it is true
    action = 'Slow down'
else:
    action = 'Stop'

# Display the action to take
print(f"The action to take is: {action}")
```

```
# Output:
The action to take is: Slow down
```

In this example, the condition 'light_color == 'green'' doesn't explicitly say 'True' or 'False', but it evaluates to one of these boolean values. If the light is green, the condition 'light_color == 'green'' is 'True', and the action is to "Go". If the condition is 'False' (the light is not green), the code moves to the next condition to check if the light is yellow.

So, even though the conditions don't directly contain True or False, they are evaluated as such, guiding what action to take.

You can evaluate multiple conditions within a single if statement by using logical operators such as 'and', 'or', and 'not'. For example, if you want to check whether someone is a teenager based on their age being over 12 and under 19, you could write this condition using the and operator. Here's how it might look in code:

```
age = 16

# Check if the age falls within the range for a teenager
if age > 12 and age <= 18:
    print("You are a teenager.")
else:
    print("You are not a teenager.")
```

```
# Output:
You are a teenager.
```

Example 1: Write a Python program that takes an integer as input from the user. Your program should display whether the number is "Even," "Odd," or "Zero."

First, let's talk about even numbers. An even number is like a pie that you can perfectly split into two equal pieces with nothing left over. In math terms, that means if you divide it by 2, there's no remainder.

Now, what about odd numbers? An odd number is like a pie that, when you try to split it into two equal pieces, leaves you with a little piece left over. In math, this 'leftover' is a remainder of 1 when you divide the number by 2.

Zero is a bit unique. It's not really even or odd in the traditional sense. But for this exercise, we're giving zero its own special bucket.

So, to sum up: If a number divides by 2 with no remainder, it's even. If it divides by 2 and leaves a remainder of 1, it's odd. And if the number is zero, it gets its own special label.

```
# First, let's ask the user to give us a number to work
with.
user_input = input("Please give me a number so we can
sort it into the right bucket: ")

# Now let's convert this string input into an actual
number, an integer.
number = int(user_input)

# Alright, time for some decision-making. First, let's
check if it's zero.
if number == 0:
    print("Ah, a zero! This gets its own special
category.")

# If it's not zero, let's see if it's even. Remember, an
even number has no remainder when divided by 2.
elif number % 2 == 0:
```

```
    print("This number is even! It fits perfectly when
divided by 2.")

# Finally, if it's not zero or even, then it must be odd.
else:
    print("This number is odd! It leaves a remainder
when divided by 2.")
```

In this code, we first ask the user for a number and store it in a variable called 'user_input'. We then convert this to an integer so we can do some math with it, storing the integer in a variable called 'number'. Now comes the fun part! We use an 'if-elif-else' block to decide which "bucket" our number falls into—whether it's zero, even, or odd—and then print a message to let the user know which category their number fits into.

Example 2: Write a Python program that takes three integers as input from the user. Your program should determine and display which among the three numbers is the greatest.

Determining the greatest number among three numbers may sound complicated at first, but it's actually straightforward once you break it down. We're going to use comparisons to see how these numbers stack up against each other.

Imagine you have three boxes, and each box has a number written on it. You pick up the first box and compare its number with the number on the second box. You keep the box with the bigger number and then compare it to the third box. The box you're left with will have the greatest number.

Now let's translate that into Python. We can use if, elif, and else statements to make these comparisons. We'll start by comparing the first and the second number. The bigger one is then compared with the third number, and that's how we find out which one is the greatest.

Here's how you could write the Python code for this:

- First, ask the user to enter three numbers, one by one.
- Use if statements to compare the first number with the second, keeping the greater one in mind.
- Next, compare the greater number from the first step with the third number.
- Whichever number comes out on top is the greatest of the three!

By breaking down the problem into these smaller steps, you'll find that determining the greatest number among three is pretty straightforward!

```python
# Step 1: Ask the user to enter three numbers, one by
one.
num1 = int(input("Please enter the first number: "))
num2 = int(input("Please enter the second number: "))
num3 = int(input("Please enter the third number: "))

# Step 2: Compare the first number with the second to
find the greater one.
if num1 > num2:
    greatest = num1
else:
    greatest = num2

# Step 3: Compare the greater number from the first
comparison with the third number.
if num3 > greatest:
    greatest = num3

# Step 4: Display the greatest number among the three.
print(f"The greatest number among the three is
{greatest}.")
```

In this code, we first ask the user to input three numbers, storing them in variables 'num1', 'num2', and 'num3'. We then use an 'if-else' statement to compare 'num1' and 'num2', storing the greater number in a new variable called 'greatest'. Next, we use another 'if' statement to compare the greatest with 'num3'. If num3 is greater than 'greatest', we update 'greatest' to hold the value of 'num3'. Finally, we print out the greatest number.

Example 3: Write a Python program that takes a single alphabet character as input from the user. Your program should determine and display whether the character is a "Vowel" or a "Consonant."

When it comes to the English alphabet, each letter is either a vowel or a consonant. The vowels are 'a', 'e', 'i', 'o', and 'u'. All other alphabets are considered consonants.

In Python, you can do this using an if-else statement. You'll first ask the user for a single letter. Then, you'll check if that letter is in the list of vowels ('a', 'e', 'i', 'o', 'u'). Don't forget to consider

both uppercase and lowercase versions. If it is, your program will say it's a vowel. Otherwise, it'll say it's a consonant.

Here's how you could code this in Python:

- First, ask the user to input a single alphabet character.
- Use an if statement to check if the letter is in the list of vowels.
- If it is, print out that it's a vowel.

- If it's not, use an else statement to print out that it's a consonant.

By following these steps, you'll be able to categorize any given alphabet character as either a vowel or a consonant!

```python
# Create a list containing all vowels (lowercase for simplicity)
vowels_list = ['a', 'e', 'i', 'o', 'u']

# Step 1: Ask the user to input a single alphabet character.
char = input("Please enter a single alphabet character: ")

# Convert the character to lowercase to make the comparison case-insensitive
char_lower = char.lower()

# Step 2: Use an 'if' statement to check if the letter is in the vowels list.
if char_lower in vowels_list:
    print("The character is a Vowel.")

# Step 3: Use an 'else' statement to print that it's a consonant.
else:
```

```
print("The character is a Consonant.")
```

If you're finding it challenging to grasp the concept behind the statement 'char_lower in vowels_list', it might be helpful to revisit the topic of membership operators, covered in Lesson 7. This will provide you with a better understanding of how 'in' works to check if a value exists within a list or other iterable data structures.

8

L o o p

P icture a circular playground where you start your jog at location "A" and complete the circle by returning to the same point. This completes one loop, which you can repeat as often as you wish. To keep track, you might use a counter, or else you could lose count. Imagine you've been jotting down your loop count on a notepad after each completion. When you finally look at the notepad, you see the number 5 written down. Counting from 0—0, 1, 2, 3, 4, 5—you realize you've completed the loop six times.

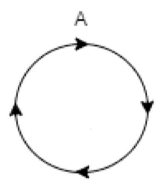

A

What are we essentially doing here? We're repeating the same action multiple times. In Python, when we need to carry out repetitive tasks, we use loops. Python offers two main types of loops: the "for loop" and the "while loop."

But before we delve into these loops, let's first understand the concepts of iteration, iteration variables, and iteration objects.

Iteration, Iterable Object, Iteration Variable

Iteration is doing the same thing over and over again in a loop.

We've already run around the field six times, which is an example of iteration. In this case, the field serves as the "iterable object," meaning it's the setting where we can perform the task repeatedly.

The one who is running on the field acts as the "iterator" or "iteration variable," responsible for each round of the repetitive action. The variable commonly used in loops named "i," serves as the iteration variable. It's like a counter that keeps track of how many times you've gone through the loop or which item in a sequence you're currently working with.

For Loop

Remember how, as kids, we repeatedly wrote the same sentence to improve our handwriting? That was a repetitive task, wasn't it? If only we'd known about programming back then, we could have made those repetitive tasks much easier!

Now let's accomplish the same task, but more efficiently, using Python and a 'for' loop. we will write the sentence 'The quick brown fox jumps over the lazy dog' 10 times.

```python
for i in range(10):
    print("A quick brown fox jumps over the lazy dog")
```

```
# Output:
A quick brown fox jumps over the lazy dog
A quick brown fox jumps over the lazy dog
A quick brown fox jumps over the lazy dog
A quick brown fox jumps over the lazy dog
A quick brown fox jumps over the lazy dog
A quick brown fox jumps over the lazy dog
A quick brown fox jumps over the lazy dog
A quick brown fox jumps over the lazy dog
```

> A quick brown fox jumps over the lazy dog
>
> A quick brown fox jumps over the lazy dog

In this example, we instructed Python to print the sentence 10 times. But how did we achieve that? Let's dissect the code to understand it better.

1. 'for i in range(10):': This line sets up a for loop using the 'range(10)' function. The 'range(10)' generates a series of numbers from 0 to 9. The variable 'i' iterates through each of these numbers, although we don't explicitly use 'i' within the loop itself. It simply acts as a placeholder to dictate how many times the loop should run, which in this case is 10 times.

2. 'print("A quick brown fox jumps over the lazy dog")': Inside the body of the for loop, we have this 'print()' statement. Each time the loop iterates, this line is executed, printing the sentence "A quick brown fox jumps over the lazy dog" to the console.

When the program runs, it follows these steps:

- The loop starts with the first value in the range, which is i = 0.
- The print() statement is executed, printing the sentence.
- The loop moves to the next value, i = 1.
- The sentence is printed again.

- This cycle continues until i = 9, which is the last value in the range(10).

Once all 10 iterations are complete, the loop ends, having printed the sentence 10 times, each on a new line.

range()

There we've generated an iterable object using the range() function. How does it work?

You'll notice we've placed a value inside the function, as in range(10). This is how we specify the number of times the loop should run.

```
print(range(10))
# Output:
range(0, 10)
```

You can see, if you execute the statement 'print(range(10))', you won't see the numbers from 0 to 9 displayed directly. Instead, you'll see something like 'range(0, 10)' printed.

Why does this happen? The 'range()' function doesn't actually create a list of numbers; it creates a "range object." This object is iterable, meaning you can loop over it to produce the numbers from '0 to 9', but the numbers are not stored in memory all at once. This is more memory-efficient when you're dealing with large ranges.

To visualize the numbers in the range, you can convert it to a list using the list() function and then print it:

```
print(list(range(10)))
# Output:
[0, 1, 2, 3, 4, 5, 6, 7, 8, 9]
```

Now you see that a list of ten numbers has been printed, ranging from 0 to 10. This illustrates the sequence of values that the variable "i" will hold, one at a time, ending with 9.

Multiply by 3

A multiple of 3 is any number that can be evenly divided by 3 without leaving a remainder. In other words, if you can multiply 3 by some integer (positive, negative, or zero) to get the number, then that number is a multiple of 3.

For example, some multiples of 3 are:

3 (3 x 1)

6 (3 x 2)

9 (3 x 3)

12 (3 x 4)

15 (3 x 5)

18 (3 x 6)

... and so on.

You can also have negative multiples of 3, like -3, -6, -9, etc.

Now, let's accomplish this using a loop. Our objective is to print the numbers between 0 and 10 that are multiples of 3.

```
for i in range(11):  # Loop from 0 to 10
    if i % 3 == 0:  # Check if the number is a multiple of 3
        print(i)

# Output:
0
3
6
9
```

let's break down how the code works:

1. 'for i in range(11):': This line initiates a for loop that will iterate through each number from 0 to 10 (11 is not included). The variable 'i' will take on each of these values one at a time.

2. 'if i % 3 == 0:': Inside the loop, we have an if statement that uses the modulo operator '%'. This operator returns the remainder when 'i' is divided by 3. If the remainder is '0', that means 'i' is a multiple of '3'.

3. 'print(i)': If the 'if' condition is met (i.e., 'i' is a multiple of 3), then the program will print the value of 'i'.

So when you run the code:

- The loop starts with 'i' = 0.
- It checks whether 'i' is a multiple of 3. In this case, it is, so it prints '0'.
- Then 'i' becomes 1, which is not a multiple of 3, so nothing is printed.
- Next, 'i' becomes 2, then 3, and so on, up to 10.

Whenever 'i' is a multiple of 3 (like 3, 6, 9), the program prints it. Finally, when 'i' reaches 10 and the loop has gone through all numbers in the specified range, the loop ends.

range(start, stop, step)

- start: Specifies the starting point of the sequence. The default value is 0.
- stop: Specifies the stopping point of the sequence. This

value is not included in the sequence itself.

- step: Specifies the difference between each number in the sequence, essentially defining the "steps" between each number. The default value is 1.

Here are some examples to illustrate:

- 'range(5)' generates 0, 1, 2, 3, 4. (Starts at 0, stops at 4, steps of 1)
- 'range(2, 9)' generates 2, 3, 4, 5, 6, 7, 8. (Starts at 2, stops at 8, steps of 1)
- 'range(1, 10, 2)' generates 1, 3, 5, 7, 9. (Starts at 1, stops at 9, steps of 2)
- 'range(10, 0, -1)' generates 10, 9, 8, 7, 6, 5, 4, 3, 2, 1. (Starts at 10, stops at 1, steps of -1)

Remember, the stop value is not included in the generated sequence, and if you want to use negative steps, the start should be greater than stop.

It's a versatile function that allows for great flexibility when you're setting up loops.

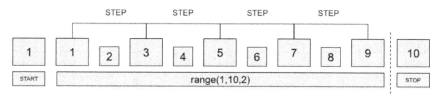

Now, We can write the code:

```
for i in range(1,10,2):
    print(i)
# Output:
1
3
5
7
9
```

Also, we can decrease the value:

```
for i in range(10,1,-2):
    print(i)
# Output:
10
8
6
4
2
```

Here, 'for i in range(10, 1, -2)', the range() function generates a sequence of numbers that starts at 10, stops before 1, and decrements by 2 each time.

If we want to visualize the behavior of a for loop, it would appear as follows:

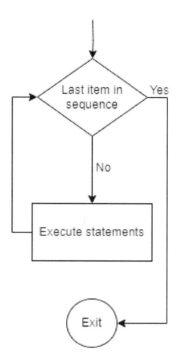

Other iterable objects

You've already learned about lists, tuples, dictionaries, and strings. These are all iterable objects, meaning you can loop through them. To demonstrate, let's create a simple list and use a loop to print each item in it.

```
list = [5,6,7,8]

for item in list:
    print(item)
```

```
# Output:
5
6
7
8
```

I've previously mentioned that the role of an iterable variable is to hold values one at a time in a sequence. In this example, that variable is 'item'. Our list has 4 numbers, so the loop will run 4 times. During each iteration, the value from the list will be stored in the 'item' variable, which is then printed out.

Let's explore how iteration works with strings:

```
string = 'book'

for item in string:
    print(item)
```
```
# Output:
b
o
o
k
```

While Loop

You might recall that we've already covered one type of loop: the 'for' loop. So, why are we learning about another kind of loop? The reason is that in a 'for' loop, we typically know in advance how many times the loop will run. But what if the situation calls for a different condition?

Suppose I ask someone to enter a password, and I want them to keep trying until they get it right. In this situation, we're repeating the same task over and over, which calls for a loop. However, we don't know how many times the loop needs to run; the user might get the password correct on the first try or after 100 attempts. This is a scenario where a 'while' loop would be useful. That said, if we did know the number of iterations in advance, we could still opt to use a 'while' loop.

While loop Syntax

```
while condition:
    statements
```

Have a look at the diagram:

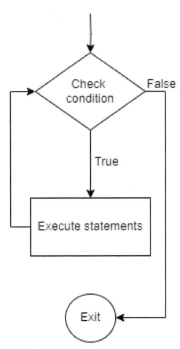

Examine the bellow program. Initially, the variable 'i' is set to 0. Following that, a 'while' loop is implemented with the condition 'i < 5'. This signifies that the loop will execute five times.

```
i = 0

while i < 10:
    print('hello', i)
    i += 1
```

```
# Output:
hello 0
hello 1
hello 2
```

```
hello 3
hello 4
hello 5
hello 6
hello 7
hello 8
hello 9
```

Here is a breakdown for each iteration:

First Iteration (i=0):

The loop starts with i set to 0. It checks if i < 10, which is true. The string "hello 0" is printed. Then, i is incremented by 1, making i=1.

Second Iteration (i=1):

The loop checks if i < 10 again. Still true. The string "hello 1" is printed. i becomes 2.

Third Iteration (i=2):

Once again, the loop checks if i < 10. True. The string "hello 2" is printed. i is incremented to 3.

Fourth Iteration (i=3):

The condition i < 10 is checked and is true. The string "hello 3" is printed. i is incremented to 4.

Fifth Iteration (i=4):

The loop checks the condition i < 10, finds it true, and prints "hello 4". Then i becomes 5.

Sixth Iteration (i=5):

The loop runs again, finds that i < 10 is true, prints "hello 5", and increments i to 6.

Seventh Iteration (i=6):

The loop checks i < 10, finds it to be true, prints "hello 6", and then increments i to 7.

Eighth Iteration (i=7):

Once again, the loop finds i < 10 to be true, prints "hello 7", and increments i to 8.

Ninth Iteration (i=8):

The loop checks the condition, finds it true, prints "hello 8", and i becomes 9.

Tenth Iteration (i=9):

For the last time, the loop checks i < 10, finds it true, prints "hello 9", and increments i to 10.

After the tenth iteration, i becomes 10. Now, the condition i < 10 is false, so the loop terminates.

Password matching

the password issue we discussed earlier could be implemented using a while loop in Python. The loop will continue running until the correct password is entered by the user. Here's a simple example to demonstrate this:

```python
# Initialize a preset password
correct_password = "secret"

# Initialize an empty string for the user's input
user_input = ""

# Initialize the condition variable as True
condition = True

# Start the while loop; it will run as long as condition is
True
while condition:
    # Ask the user to enter the password
    user_input = input("Please enter the password: ")

    # Check if the entered password is correct
    if user_input == correct_password:
        print("Correct password! Access granted.")
        condition = False  # Set condition to False to exit
the loop
    else:
```

```
    print("Incorrect password. Please try again.")

    # The loop will exit once condition becomes False
```

the code uses a while loop to repeatedly ask for a password until the correct one is entered.

We start with a known good password (correct_password = "secret").

The condition variable starts as True to keep the loop running.

Inside the loop, the user is prompted to enter a password (user_input).

If the entered password matches the correct one, condition is set to False, and the loop stops.

So basically, the loop keeps running until you enter the correct password, at which point it exits.

Factorial

A factorial is a mathematical operation that takes a non-negative integer

$n!$

n and multiplies it by every positive integer less than itself. The factorial function is denoted by

$n!$

For example, the factorial of 5 is calculated as:

$5! = 5 \times 4 \times 3 \times 2 \times 1 = 120$

Factorials grow very quickly as n becomes large. They are frequently used in mathematics and computer science, particularly in combinations and permutations, algorithmic complexity calculations, and other areas where multiplication of a sequence of numbers is necessary.

We will write a code that will ask a number from user and calculate the factorial.

```python
# Ask for user input
n = int(input("Enter a non-negative integer to find its factorial: "))

# Initialize variables
result = 1
i = 1

# Calculate factorial using a while loop
while i <= n:
    result *= i
    i += 1

# Display the result
print(f"The factorial of {n} is {result}")
```

Let's say n=5:

```python
n = int(5)
```

```
# Initialize variables
result = 1
i = 1

# Calculate factorial using a while loop
while i <= n:
    result *= i
    i += 1

# Display the result
print(f"The factorial of {n} is {result}")
```

```
# Output:
The factorial of 5 is 120
```

here are the steps to understand the code:

User Input: The code prompts the user to enter a non-negative integer. This integer is stored in a variable called 'n'. Here, n=5.

Initialize Variables: Two variables are initialized: result is set to '1' to serve as the starting point for the factorial calculation, and 'i' is set to '1' to act as the counter for the loop.

Calculate Factorial using a while Loop: A while loop runs as long as 'i' is less than or equal to 'n'. Inside the loop, the code multiplies the current value of 'i' with result to update result.

After that, 'i' is incremented by 1.

Display the Result: Once the loop ends, the final value of result will be the factorial of the input number 'n'. This result is then displayed to the user.

Break

Imagine you're driving a car and you need to stop quickly. You'd hit the brakes, right? Similarly, in Python, there's this thing called 'break'. If you're running a loop and you find what you're looking for or just need to stop the loop for any reason, you use 'break'. It's like telling the loop, "Hey, we're done here, let's move on!" So, instead of going around and around in the loop, the program stops that loop and proceeds to the next task.

Let's consider a scenario where you want to search for a specific number in a list. Once you find the number, there's no need to continue checking the remaining numbers in the list. The break statement can be used to exit the loop as soon as the number is found.

Here's a simple code to demonstrate this:

```
# List of numbers
numbers = [1, 3, 5, 7, 9, 11, 13, 15, 17]
```

```
# Number we want to search for
target = 11

# Loop to search for the number
for number in numbers:
    if number == target:
        print(f"Found the number {target}!")
        break
    else:
        print(f"{number} is not the number we're looking
for.")

print("Loop finished!")
```

```
# Output:
1 is not the number we're looking for.
3 is not the number we're looking for.
5 is not the number we're looking for.
7 is not the number we're looking for.
9 is not the number we're looking for.
Found the number 11!
Loop finished!
```

In this code, once the number 11 is found, the loop will stop, and it won't check the numbers 13, 15, and 17, thus saving processing time. Without the break statement, the loop would continue checking all numbers even after finding the target number.

Searching

You have already seen the above code. What did we do? We actually searched for an item by matching its value with the elements present in the list. This act of seeking out a specific item by comparing it with others is fundamental in programming and is known as item searching.

In our code, we performed a Linear Search. In this approach, we start at the beginning of the list and check elements one by one. We iterate over each item, and when our target item matches any of the items in the list, we know we've found it. The break statement is employed to exit the loop immediately once the item is found, ensuring we don't waste any more time checking the remaining elements. This straightforward approach is effective, especially for shorter lists or when you don't have prior knowledge about the order or distribution of items in the list.

Let's consider a situation where we have a list of students and we want to search for a specific student's name.

```
# List of student names
students = ["Alice", "Bob", "Charlie", "Diana", "Ella", "Frank"]
```

```
# Name we want to search for
target_name = "Diana"

# Loop to search for the student's name
found = False
for student in students:
    if student == target_name:
        print(f"Found the student: {target_name}!")
        found = True
        break

if not found:
    print(f"{target_name} is not in the list.")
```

```
# Output:
Found the student: Diana!
```

In this example, the loop will go through the names in the list. When it finds the name "Diana", it will print out the confirmation message and exit the loop using the break statement. If it doesn't find the name by the end of the list, the message indicating the name was not found will be displayed.

Continue

The continue statement is a control flow tool in programming. When encountered, it causes the current iteration of a loop to end immediately, and the next iteration of the loop begins.

Instead of exiting the loop entirely (like break), it simply skips the rest of the current iteration and moves on to the next one.

Imagine we have a list of numbers, and we want to print only the even numbers. If an odd number is encountered, we skip its print operation and move on.

```python
numbers = [1, 2, 3, 4, 5, 6]

for num in numbers:
    if num % 2 != 0:  # Check if the number is odd
        continue
    print(f"{num} is even.")

# Output:
2 is even.
4 is even.
6 is even.
```

In this example, when the continue statement is encountered upon detecting an odd number, the loop skips the print statement for that iteration and proceeds to the next number in the list.

Filtering

See the list below:

```
list = ['w', 'f', 'B', '3', 'T', '8', 'q', '5', '7']
```

In this list, we have various characters, and we want to distinguish the numeric strings from the others. The isnumeric() method becomes particularly useful in such scenarios. When applied to a string, it returns True if the string represents a number and False otherwise.

Checking 'isnumeric()':

```
print('3'.isnumeric())  # Output: True
print('w'.isnumeric())  # Output: False
```

Now, let's filter the list based on the isnumeric() method:

```
list = ['w', 'f', 'B', '3', 'T', '8', 'q', '5', '7']

for item in list:
    if item.isnumeric() == False:
        print(item)
# Output:
w
f
B
T
q
```

9

F u n c t i o n s

I magine four friends, A, B, C, and D, who decide to build a house together. To manage this project efficiently, they divide the work based on their skills and responsibilities. Friend A is tasked with buying raw materials like bricks and cement. Friend B takes on the role of managing finances and calculating expenses. Friend C is responsible for designing the house, bringing an architectural perspective. Finally, Friend D oversees the entire operation, ensuring everything runs smoothly.

In Python, when you're working on a big project, you can use these special helpers, or functions, to take care of different parts of your project. Just like how each friend had a different job in building the house, each Python function does one specific thing to help you with your project. This way, your big project becomes like a fun game with different helpers making it easier and more fun to finish!

Python comes with some ready-made functions that are designed for specific tasks, and we've used a few of them in our earlier chapters. Functions like print(), input(), and max() are examples of these built-in functions. They're like tools that Python gives you right from the start. But what's really cool is that you can also create your own tools, or functions, for jobs you need to do. These are called user-defined functions. It's like making your own special gadget to do exactly what you want!

Function Definition

In Python, when we want to make our own function, we start with the word 'def'. This tells Python, "Hey, I'm about to create a new function!" After 'def', we give our function a name, and put parentheses next to it. Inside these parentheses, we can put some extra information if we need to. Then, we write our code that tells the function what to do. At the end, the function can send back a value to a specific place if we want it to.

```
def function_name():
    // Code

    return value
```

Let's write a simple Python code that reflects our building

analogy with the four friends. In this code, we'll create functions for each friend's task in the house-building process.

```
def buy_materials():
    print("A buys bricks and cement.")

def manage_funds():
    print("B calculates expenses and manages
funds.")
    calculated_funds = "10,000 dollars"   #
Example value
    return calculated_funds

def design_house():
    print("C designs the house.")

def oversee_project():
    print("D oversees the entire project.")

def build_house():
    buy_materials()
    funds = manage_funds()
    design_house()
    oversee_project()
    print(f"The house is built with a budget
of {funds}.")

# Start the building process
build_house()
```

In this code, each function (buy_materials, manage_funds, design_house, oversee_project) represents the task of a friend. The build_house function calls all these functions in order, showing how each friend contributes to the house-building process. When you run build_house(), it will print messages showing what each friend is doing and that the house is being built. This code is a simple way to understand how functions in Python can work together to complete a big task.

Function Calling

In the example above we've discussed, build_house is the main function, acting like the project manager of the house-building process. It calls on the other functions to do their jobs, similar to how a project manager coordinates tasks in a real construction project. The function calls are like instructions: "Hey A, get the materials!" and so on. Each function is identified by its name and gets to work when it's called upon.

However, there's a key point to consider: A needs money to buy materials, and this money is managed by B. So, logically, we should first get the funds from B before A can start purchasing materials. The sequence of calling functions should reflect this dependency. Let's revise the code to match this flow:

```python
def manage_funds():
    print("B calculates expenses and manages
funds.")
    funds = "10,000 dollars"  # Example
amount
    return funds
```

```
def buy_materials(funds):
    print(f"A uses {funds} to buy bricks and
cement.")

def design_house():
    print("C designs the house.")

def oversee_project():
    print("D oversees the entire project.")

def build_house():
    funds = manage_funds()
    buy_materials(funds)
    design_house()
    oversee_project()
    print("The house is built
successfully.")

# Start the building process
build_house()
```

In this updated code:

1. The manage_funds function is called first to ensure that the budget is ready.

2. The buy_materials function now takes an argument, funds, which represents the money provided by B.

3. The sequence of function calls in build_house starts with manage_funds, followed by buy_materials, ensuring A has the funds needed to buy materials.

4. The design_house and oversee_project functions follow,

reflecting the sequential steps in the building process.

Why Functions?

In Python, the concept of functions is akin to the delegation of tasks in the construction of a building. Just as constructing a building involves different specialists handling different aspects of the construction, functions in programming are used to handle specific parts of a larger task.

For instance, consider the scenario where a team is building a house. One person is responsible for procuring materials, another for managing the budget, a third for designing the structure, and a fourth for overseeing the entire operation. This division of labor makes the process more efficient, as each team member focuses on their area of expertise. Similarly, in a programming context, functions allow a coder to break down a complex problem into smaller, more manageable pieces.

When a programmer writes a function, they are essentially creating a small, self-contained block of code designed to perform a specific task. Once written, this function can be used repeatedly throughout the program. This is much like how a construction team might have a specific process for laying bricks. Once they have established an efficient method, they use the same process for every part of the building that requires bricklaying.

Moreover, if a change is needed in the process, perhaps a new way of managing funds in our building analogy or a different method for a task in a program, the change only needs to be made in one place — in the function itself. This is far more efficient than having to make adjustments in multiple places throughout the entire project.

In addition, functions enhance collaboration. In our building example, different experts bring their skills to different parts of the project, and in programming, different functions can be written and maintained by different members of a team. This not only divides the workload but also brings in varied expertise for different aspects of the project.

Examples

Adding two numbers using function

We'll write a simple function called **add_numbers** that takes two numbers as input and returns their sum.

```
def add_numbers(number1, number2):
    # Explain the action in a simple way
    print("Let's add two numbers together!")

    # Add the numbers and directly print the result
    print("The sum of", number1, "and", number2, "is:",
```

```
number1 + number2)

# Use the function to add two numbers
add_numbers(2, 3)
```

In this code:

- We define a function called add_numbers that takes two parameters, number1 and number2.
- Inside the function, we first print a message to explain what the function will do.
- Then, we calculate the sum of number1 and number2 and store it in a variable called sum.
- We print another message showing the two numbers being added and their sum to help children visualize the addition process.
- Finally, the function returns the sum of the two numbers.

Odd and Even

```
def check_odd_even(number):
    # Explain the task
    print("Let's find out if a number is odd or even!")

    # Check if the number is even
```

```
if number % 2 == 0:
    print("The number", number, "is even.")
else:
    # If it's not even, then it's odd
    print("The number", number, "is odd.")


# Use the function to check a number
check_odd_even(5)
```

In this example:

- The function **check_odd_even** is defined with one parameter, **number**.
- It begins with a print statement that introduces the task in a simple way.
- The function uses the modulo operator (**%**) to divide the number by 2 and check the remainder. If the remainder is 0, the number is even; otherwise, the number is odd.

Excersise Questions

1. Create variables for your favorite color, number, and food. Print a sentence using these variables to describe your favorites.

2. Write a program that asks for two numbers and then prints their sum, difference, product, and quotient.

3. Create variables for a character's name, age, and favorite activity. Use these variables to print a short story about the character.

4. Use a loop to count down from 5 to 1, printing each number and a favorite animal alongside it. For example, "5 elephants!"

5. Create a variable for today's weather and print a message advising what to wear based on the weather (e.g., sunny, rainy).

6. Create a list of fruits and use a loop to print each fruit in the list. Try adding a new fruit to the list and printing the list again.

7. Write a program that stores a magic number in a variable and then asks the user to guess the number. Tell the user if they're right or wrong.

8. Ask the user to input a word, and then write a program that counts and prints the number of letters in the word.

9. Write a function that takes a name and age and prints a personalized birthday message.

10. Create a list of places you'd like to visit. Use a loop to

print "I want to visit [place]" for each place in the list.

11. Use loops to print shapes (like squares, triangles) using asterisks (*) or other characters.

12. Write a function that checks if a number is even or odd. Print an appropriate message for each case.

13. Create a function that takes an age in years and converts it into days (ignore leap years), then prints the result.

14. Write a program that asks for 3 grades, stores them in a list, sorts the list from highest to lowest, and then prints the sorted grades.

15. Create a dictionary with pet names as keys and the type of animal as values. Print out each pet and its type.

16. Write a function that prints the multiplication table (up to 10) for a given number.

17. Write a program that takes a few sentences of a story and stores each sentence in a list. Then, shuffle the sentences and print the shuffled story.

18. Create a list of words. Pick a random word from the list and have the user guess letters in the word until they get it right.

19. Write a function that takes a list of activities and times (as tuples) and prints out a schedule for the day.

20. Create a simple grid (list of lists) and place a "treasure" in one of the grid squares. Write a program that asks the user to guess where the treasure is.

References

1.   Lutz, M. (2013). Learning Python (5th ed.). O'Reilly Media.

2.   weigart, A. (2015). Automate the boring stuff with Python: Practical programming for total beginners. No Starch Press.

3.   Pilgrim, M., & Willison, S. (2009). Dive into Python 3. Apress.

4.   Severance, C. (2016). Python for Everybody: Exploring Data in Python 3. CreateSpace Independent Publishing Platform.

5.   Shaw, Z. A. (2017). Learn Python 3 the Hard Way: A Very Simple Introduction to the Terrifyingly Beautiful World of Computers and Code. Addison-Wesley Professional.

Thank you for taking the time to journey through this book with me. I hope that as you've learned Python, you've started to see the world in a new light—spotting the logic, patterns, and endless possibilities that programming brings to life. But remember, this is just the first step. The world of coding is vast, full of challenges and rewards waiting to be discovered.

As you continue on your path, I encourage you to stay curious, keep experimenting, and most importantly, keep creating. The joy of programming lies in its endless potential—there's always something new to build, a problem to solve, or a skill to master. If this book has been a helpful companion on your journey, I would truly appreciate it if you left a review. It could be the nudge someone else needs to start their own adventure in coding. And if you know a friend who might benefit from learning Python, please share this book with them.

Our journey together has just begun, and I can't wait to see what you'll create next. Until we meet again in the next version, happy coding!

www.ingramcontent.com/pod-product-compliance
Lightning Source LLC
LaVergne TN
LVHW051336050326
832903LV00031B/3564